ADULTS

THE GREAT BRITISH
BAKE OFF

LEARN *to* BAKE

80 easy recipes for all the family

LINDA COLLISTER

Foreword by
MARY BERRY

BOOKS

10 9 8 7 6 5 4 3 2 1

Published in 2012 by BBC Books, an imprint of Ebury Publishing. A Random House Group Company

The Great British Bake Off is produced for BBC TWO by Love Productions.

Executive Producers: Anna Beattie, Kieran Smith
Series Editor: Amanda Westwood
Series Director: Scott Tankard
Production Manager: Nina Richards
Head of Production: Letty Kavanagh
BBC Commissioning Executive: Emma Willis

Foreword © Mary Berry 2012
Text and recipes by Linda Collister © Love Productions 2012
Design © Woodlands Books Ltd 2012
Photography © Maja Smend and Chris Terry 2012
Illustrations © www.thisisrude.com and
Oscar@KJA-artists.com © Woodlands Books Ltd 2012

The Random House Group Limited Reg. No. 954009

Addresses for companies within the Random House Group can be found at www.randomhouse.co.uk

A CIP catalogue record for this book is available from the British Library.

ISBN 978 1 849 90541 1

The Random House Group Limited supports the Forest Stewardship Council® (FSC®), the leading international forest certification organisation. All our titles that are printed on Greenpeace approved FSC® certified paper carry the FSC® logo.

Our paper procurement policy can be found at www.randomhouse.co.uk/environment

Commissioning Editor: Muna Reyal
Project Editor: Laura Higginson
Copyeditor: Norma MacMillan
Designer: Smith & Gilmour
Photography: Maja Smend and Chris Terry
Food Styling: Anna Jones, Emily Ezekiel and Richard Harris
Prop Styling: Tony Hutchinson and Marisa Daly
Production: Rebecca Jones

Colour origination by Altaimage, London
Printed and bound in the UK by Butler Tanner and Dennis Ltd

To buy books by your favourite authors and register for offers, visit www.randomhouse.co.uk

Acknowledgements
BBC Books and Love Productions would like to thank everyone involved who worked incredibly hard to make this book possible. We would particularly like to thank all the models that kindly volunteered their time for this book: Amber, Amy, Ben, Dabaye, Ella Bo, Fleur, Frankie, Freya, Grace, Harriet, Isabella, Kai, Lily, Luis, Maisy, Olivia, Oscar, Pedro, Ryan, Thomas, Urvashi, Victoria and William.

CONTENTS

FOREWORD BY MARY BERRY

Welcome bakers! If you've never baked before, then well done for picking up this book and deciding to have a go. Hopefully you will see from the recipes here how much fun baking can be. It's a great, inexpensive hobby that can be incredibly rewarding – and I should know, I've been baking for work and pleasure for quite some time now!

All of the recipes are really easy to follow and you will soon be baking cakes, biscuits and breads, and delighting your family and friends.

A few of the recipes do need adult hands – high temperatures and sharp knives can be tricky to manage by yourself. Mums and dads – if you've never baked before, this is the perfect opportunity to join in too.

Whatever your age, just have a go, enjoy the experience, but the best reward is sharing your bakes with your friends and family – they will just love you for it!

MARY BERRY

GETTING STARTED

If you have never made a cake before, this is the book for you. *Learn to Bake* is full of all the kinds of baking seen on *The Great British Bake Off* – but made simple.

Our aim is to make baking easy to understand and fun. As Mary and Paul often say, baking does need to be precise, and baking-related terminology can be mystifying if it's never been explained to you. So, this book is all about learning the basics.

We look at baking terms, ingredients and equipment, then some troubleshooting tips to help avoid baking mishaps.

But if you do have a baking disaster, don't be put off. It happens to everyone – think about the soggy pastry cases and flat sponges that haunt *The Great British Bake Off* bakers. And it's easy to improve – just keep trying, learn how your oven works best, weigh your ingredients carefully and make notes for next time.

To get you started, the recipes in this book don't need fancy or expensive ingredients. In each chapter we look at the main techniques you need and guide you through, step by step.

In Cakes, we look at four baking methods. The first is the 'all-in-one method' (a favourite of Mary Berry), where all the cake ingredients are added to one bowl and beaten until light and fluffy.

The second method is the 'creaming method'. This one has a few more stages – first you beat the soft butter and sugar together before folding in the eggs and flour.

In both methods, it's all about getting air into the cake mixture to ensure the cake rises beautifully as it bakes.

The third method in this chapter is the 'melting method', where the butter and sugar are melted together before being mixed with the remaining ingredients. It's a technique most often used to make chewy, gooey recipes such as brownies and gingerbreads, and appears in later chapters too for making biscuits and flapjacks.

Finally, there is the 'whisking method'. We use this to make light sponges such as Swiss Rolls, which are made from eggs, sugar and plain flour – so no raising agents. The whisking develops the structure to ensure the sponge rises as it bakes.

Once you've got to grips with these methods, you'll find they crop up again in many other types of baking.

Pastry and Bread have their own sets of techniques and terms, but once you've tried a simple pastry or bread recipe, they will make more sense. In Pastry, you will learn to how 'bake blind', and in Bread you will be 'kneading', 'proving', 'knocking back' (or as Paul calls it, 'punching down') and working the dough.

Finally in Puddings, we tackle meringues, pancakes, cheesecakes and even soufflés. You'll learn how to whisk egg whites into 'soft peaks' and 'stiff peaks' and then fold them to bake divine sweet treats.

You'll also see an * in the ingredients lists and recipe methods throughout the book. These black asterisks indicate that more information is available at the front of the book in 'Baking Terms Explained'. If there is a page reference, there will also be step-by-step photos to help you as well. Once you've learned the technique, you won't need to cross-reference again (or you'll just need to turn to the front every now and then to refresh your memory).

KEY BAKING INGREDIENTS

Most of these bakes use easy, simple ingredients and it's worth keeping them in the store cupboard so you're always able to whip something up.

FLOUR

Plain flour is made from wheat with a low gluten content (one of the key ingredients for making bread). It is ideal for making sponges, cakes and pastries where you want a soft or crumbly light texture.

Self-raising flour is plain flour plus chemical raising agents. These produce bubbles of carbon dioxide gas when mixed with a liquid which make the mixture expand and rise in the heat of the oven. The structure of the flour then sets around the bubbles, trapping them, so you get light, spongy cakes.

If you only have plain flour, you can turn it into self-raising flour by mixing in baking powder (you will need 4 teaspoons for 230g of flour).

Plain and self-raising flour can be white, fine wholemeal (which contains tiny flecks of bran and bakes to a light brown colour) and spelt, a variation of wheat which has a nuttier taste and can be a creamy white or light brown colour.

'Strong' bread flour is what you should use for bread making because it has extra gluten. When you work bread dough, the gluten becomes stretchy. As the yeast in bread makes air bubbles, the bread grows and the stretchiness of the gluten gives the dough strength to rise. Look out for wholemeal and spelt, as well as flours with added grains and flakes, or malted wheat, which add extra flavour, texture and colour to bread doughs.

Cornflour is not made from wheat, but is a fine white powder made from corn. It makes biscuits and cakes lighter and is also used to thicken sauces and fillings.

SUGAR

Caster sugar (white or golden) is the best sugar to use for baking cakes and cookies, as the tiny crystals break down easily during creaming and beating.

Granulated sugar has much larger crystals, which are less easily dissolved, and these can give your sponge a speckled look, and pastry or cookies a gritty texture.

Soft light and **dark brown muscovado sugars** have not been as heavily 'refined' (processed), as caster and granulated sugar, so they add a toffee flavour to cake mixtures. But they can also make cakes heavy as they are much more moist.

Demerara sugar has large brown crystals, good for adding a crunch to crumbles and toppings, but not good for cake making.

Golden syrup and **black treacle** are for sticky, melted recipes like gingerbreads and cakes that need a moist texture. If you use them in a recipe instead of sugar you may end up with a soggy result.

RAISING AGENTS

Bicarbonate of soda (which is alkaline), **cream of tartar** (which is acidic) and **baking powder** (which is a mixture of bicarbonate of soda and cream of tartar, making it both alkaline and acidic) are all chemicals that, added in small amounts, make bubbles of gas in cake mixtures, biscuit doughs and batters so they turn out light and airy instead of dense and solid.

Yeast is a living organism. It makes bread rise, gives it taste and texture and that wonderful aroma of freshly baked bread.

Yeasts need to 'feed' on the carbohydrates in the flour as well as the moisture of the damp dough and the air that you work in when you knead. As they multiply they produce tiny bubbles of carbon dioxide plus alcohol, which evaporates in the oven.

Crumble in fresh yeast to a little of the measured liquid, stir until smooth then add the rest of the water/liquid. You can keep it, tightly wrapped in the fridge, for up to a week. If you want to use fresh yeast in a recipe, use double the weight of dried yeast. Instant dried yeast is available in 7g sachets that can be kept in a store cupboard. It is a very fine and dry powder that's mixed with the flour before the liquid is added.

FLAVOURINGS

Vanilla extract is a concentrated liquid made from the seeds of vanilla pods (which come from orchids), and is used in small amounts to add a special, unique flavour to sponges, biscuits and custards.

Vanilla paste is a gooey version of extract, but you can see the millions of tiny vanilla seeds in it. Vanilla essence is less strong and may be made from artificial flavouring.

Vanilla beans or **pods** look like glossy, dark brown withered string beans. To use them, slit in half along their length with the tip of a small, sharp knife and scrape out some of the tiny brown specks – the seeds.

Spices like ground ginger, ground cinnamon and mixed spice add a warm flavour and aroma to biscuits and cakes. But once you've opened them, they quickly lose their power so buy in small amounts and remember to keep them tightly sealed.

Dried fruit and **nuts** are best bought when you need them so they don't go hard (dried fruit) or stale and nasty-tasting (nuts).

CHOCOLATE

Chocolate is made from cocoa beans which are roasted and ground up, then mixed with sugar and gently and carefully stirred and melted until very smooth.

Dark chocolate has the strongest taste because it's made with the most cocoa solids (which is the strong dry part of the bean) and just a little sugar. Many recipes suggest you use chocolate with around 70% cocoa solids, some suggest less. Use the cocoa solids percentage stated in the recipe otherwise your cake might be too bitter or too sweet.

Milk chocolate is made with less cocoa solids but more sugar and milk. White chocolate is made from the cocoa butter plus sugar. Cocoa butter is the fatty part of the bean, which gives all chocolate its melt-in-the mouth quality.

Cocoa is dried cocoa solids. It is a fine, brown powder with a very strong flavour that's added to give a powerful taste of chocolate to cakes, brownies and cookies.

Drinking chocolate is a mix of cocoa, milk powder and sugar and better for making into a hot drink than for cooking!

BASIC EQUIPMENT

You don't need to buy all these things at once, but as you make more recipes, you'll see that there are some key tools and tins that are used a lot.

BAKING TINS

* **Baking sheet:** a sturdy, heavy one with a slight rim is best as it won't buckle in the heat of the oven or rust. Use it for baking biscuits, bread, pastry recipes, scones and thin pizzas.
* If a recipe calls for two or more baking sheets and you only have one, you can bake your recipe in batches, but don't put the second batch straight onto a hot baking sheet. Hold the baking sheet (with oven gloves) under the cold tap for a few seconds. Dry, then re-use.
* **Cake tins:** 2 x 20.5cm sandwich tins for making sponge cakes, 20cm springclip tin for cheesecakes and deep cakes, 20.5 x 25.5cm traybake or cake tin, a 20.5cm square tin, 20 x 30cm swissroll or baking tin, 900g loaf tin (about 26 x 12.5 x 7cm) for bread and loaf cakes
* **Roasting tin:** for making pizzas as well as roasting veg
* **12-hole muffin or cup cake tray**
* **12-hole bun or mincepie tray:** slightly smaller than a muffin tray, also used for making fairy cakes
* **4-hole Yorkshire pudding tray:** it has wider shallower holes that the other trays

VERY USEFUL BAKING AIDS

* **Baking paper:** for lining baking tins and baking sheets so it's easy to lift off baked goodies.
* **Bowls:** small, medium and large mixing bowls are used in almost every recipe. Go for something unbreakable, like the cheap stainless steel bowls sold in street markets and bargain stores.
* **Hand-held electric mixer:** not essential but it saves a lot of effort when you're making cakes. You can make cakes with a wooden spoon (but it takes longer) and meringues with a rotary whisk (if you have the energy) but a mixer will be a good investment and will last many baking years.
* **Knives:** sharp knives are needed for cutting up fruit, vegetables, meat and fish, but you will only need a couple: a small one for dealing with fruit and vegetables and a larger one for chopping. Buy knives that feel comfy in your hand, not too heavy or clumsy (they don't have to cost a fortune) and keep them sharp with a safety sharpener (one of those you draw the knife through).
* You'll also need a round-bladed knife – like the one you use for spreading butter on toast and a palette knife for lifting up delicate pastries and doughs.
* A serrated tomato knife is useful (but not essential) for slicing soft fruits. A good potato or veg peeler is important too.
* **Kitchen scissors:** use for trimming pastry and other food, so buy a good pair and, for hygiene, keep them separate from household scissors used for other tasks.

* **Measuring jug:** choose one made of heatproof clear plastic or toughened glass (rather than metal or china) so you can measure accurately. One that measures at least 500ml is best. You'll also need a ruler for some recipes.

* **Plastic or rubber spatula or scraper:** used for cleaning out mixing bowls and stirring and mixing ingredients. Choose one made out of a flexible rather than a stiff and rigid material.

* **Rolling pin:** a simple wooden cylinder is the best buy, rather those with handles. Again, choose one that feels good to handle. It will last you a lifetime.

* **Spoons:** a wooden spoon is one of your most useful pieces of kit. Use it for stirring, mixing, beating and creaming. Choose one with a handle that's right for you – if it's too long it will be difficult to use. You'll also need a large metal spoon (for folding and mixing), and small, medium and large spoons (like the teaspoons and spoons you use for eating with) and a set of measuring spoons (½ teaspoon, 5ml teaspoon, and 15ml tablespoon).

* **Timer:** so you know when your cake is ready.

* **Weighing scales:** you really can't do without these because you need to be able to weigh ingredients accurately. An inexpensive set of digital scales will be a good investment.

* **Wire rack:** for cooling biscuits, cakes, breads and scones. Find a big one if possible (or use the rack from the grill pan).

NOT ESSENTIAL, BUT USEFUL

* **Cheese grater:** not just for cheese! Pick a four-sided grater with different-sized holes on each side. You can grate Cheddar cheese or carrots on the large holes and ginger, nutmeg or Parmesan cheese on the smaller holes.

* **Chopping board:** for slicing and dicing. It's vital to keep it spotlessly clean – if you have a dishwasher, choose one that can go in it.

* **Colander:** for rinsing fruit and veg. Choose one that's heatproof and with long handles, so it can be used for straining cooked veg or pasta.

* **Disposable piping bag:** even supermarkets stock these! Large ones are best for piping meringues or cake mixtures, smaller ones for decorating cakes with icing. Snip off the tip with kitchen scissors to get the opening the right size.

* **Fish slice:** metal or heatproof plastic. Useful for adding or removing food from pans and baking sheets so you don't burn your fingers.

* **Wire balloon whisk:** for mixing batters. Choose one that feels comfy in your hand and not too heavy. You could use a fork instead.

 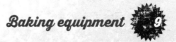

BAKING TERMS EXPLAINED

BAKING BLIND

This strange term really means baking empty. It's where you pre-bake pastry cases before adding the filling, so you end up with crisp pastry rather than a soggy bottom. Once you've rolled out the pastry, press it onto the base and sides of the tin (see page 172 for how to do this) then prick the base all over with a fork so it doesn't bubble up in the heat of the oven. The empty pastry case needs to be thoroughly chilled first – allow 20 minutes – to give it a chance to firm up so the fat or butter then melts evenly in the heat of the oven as the water turns to steam, keeping the starch grains in the flour separate.

Then, to prevent the sides of the empty pastry case from flopping in and the base from ballooning up, line the pastry with baking paper and weigh the paper down with ceramic or dried baking beans (ceramic or dried). See page 174 for pictures of how to do this. Once the pastry has set, remove the paper and beans and then put the pastry case (still in the tin) back into the oven so the pastry can dry out, crisp up and brown a bit.

The pastry case can be filled once it's cooled, then baked to cook the filling, if necessary.

BEATING

This means using a wooden spoon (or a hand-held electric whisk) in a mixing bowl to furiously work, or beat, a mixture round and round the bowl, so lots of air gets drawn into it. It's most often used in cake recipes where you need to 'gradually beat in the eggs' or 'beat the butter'. When the mixture has had the right amount of beating (2 to 5 minutes depending on your recipe) it will be paler and lighter in colour and texture because of all the tiny air bubbles.

Standing the mixing bowl on a damp cloth helps stop the bowl wobbling as you beat. And stop for a breather every minute (it's hard work beating vigorously for 5 minutes) to scrape down the sides of the bowl with a plastic (or rubber) scraper or spatula so all the mixture gets the full treatment.

Some recipes ask you to 'lightly beat' eggs before adding to a mixture or batter. This simply means blending the yolks and whites until mixed together using a metal fork.

CREAMING

Beating sugar and butter together for several minutes is called 'creaming' as you are gradually softening and breaking down the sugar grains so they dissolve in the butter, changing the texture and appearance as they draw in air. The mixture is ready when it looks much paler and creamy, smooth (rather than gritty) and fluffier and bigger (because of the air beaten in), and easily drops off your wooden spoon when you shake it.

FILLING A PIPING BAG

Put a disposable piping bag into a mug or jug (to hold it upright), then fold down the top quarter of the bag. Scrape the mixture into the bag. Unfold the top quarter and twist the bag at the top to stop the mixture escaping. Leave the bag standing in the mug (or jug) until you are ready to pipe. See page 32 for pictures of how to do this.

FINGERTIP TEST

Put on oven gloves, then remove the baking sheet/tin from the oven and set it on a heatproof surface. Gently press the centre of the cake or muffin with your fingertip. If it springs back then it's ready; if there is a small dent left, put the cake back in the oven to bake for another 2-3 minutes and test again.

FOLDING IN

When you have to combine two (or more) delicate mixtures – like adding sifted flour to creamed butter and sugar, or whisked egg whites to a soufflé, or adding ingredients to whisked egg whites for a pavlova or meringue – the lightest way to do it (so you don't knock out all the air whisked in) is 'folding'.

A large metal spoon works best so you can make the least number of 'folds': cut down through the mixture with the side of the spoon, until you touch the bottom of the bowl then turn the spoon up and draw it up through the mixture to the top of it, then flip the spoon over so the mixture flops over onto the rest in the bowl. Give the bowl a little turn so you are starting in a different place and keep cutting, lifting and folding over the mixture just until you can't see any streaks of unmixed ingredients (see page 40 for pictures of how to do this .

KNEADING

This means using your hands to work together the ingredients of a floury dough so they become properly mixed and smooth.

Pastry doughs just need a couple of seconds, but bread doughs need much longer. This is because the 'strong' flour used for bread needs to have the gluten in the grains turned into stretchy elastic strands so the bread can rise up when the air bubbles produced by the yeast expand. If the dough isn't sufficiently kneaded, the dough won't be able to support itself and could collapse in the oven.

Use both hands for kneading. First sprinkle them and your work top with a little flour so the dough doesn't stick (some recipes use oil instead) then scoop out your dough. Hold down one edge of it with one hand and use the other to stretch out the other side of the dough, then gather it all back into a ball again. Turn the ball around, so you are starting from a different spot, and start again, stretching out the dough and gathering it back in. As you keep doing this you can feel the dough changing – it will gradually feel less like a lump of dough and more bouncy (see page 136 for pictures of how to do this).

It's ready when it feels very smooth and stretchy and elastic – which will take between 5 and 10 minutes of kneading (you can take a break for 10 minutes in the middle).

KNOCKING BACK (ALSO CALLED PUNCHING DOWN)

When you've kneaded your bread dough, you then need to leave it to rise, or prove, so the yeast has time to start growing and produce lots of bubbles of carbon dioxide gas.

The dough will swell and, once it has doubled in size, it's time to move on to the next stage: shaping. To do this the dough has to be punched or knocked down with your knuckles so it is back to its original size. The yeast is still alive, but this bursts the large bubbles of gas, so the dough has a more even texture rather than some large holes amid denser areas. Of course, some breads are supposed to have large holes so they don't want the bubbles redistributed!

KNOCKING TEST (FOR BREAD)
To test to see if the bread is cooked all the way through, tip it out of the tin, then knock or rap it on the underside with your knuckles. (Be careful as the loaf will be hot.) If the loaf sounds hollow like a drum, it is cooked, but if you hear a dull thud, the middle is still damp. If it needs more cooking time, put the oven gloves back on and put the loaf back into the oven, straight onto the oven shelf, not back in its tin. Bake for a further 5 minutes, then test it again.

LOOSENING A CAKE TIN AND TURNING OUT THE CAKE
Gently push the round-bladed table knife down between the cake tin sides and the sponge, then run the knife around inside the tin to loosen the sponge. Allow the cake to cool a little in its tin before doing this – as it cools it will shrink away from the tin, making it easier to loosen.

If using sandwich tins without loose bases, leave the loosened cakes to cool and firm up for a couple of minutes. Place a wire rack next to the tins, then, wearing oven gloves, turn each tin over on the rack and shake gently to remove the sponge. Carefully lift off the tins. Peel off the lining paper and leave the cakes to cool.

To remove a bake from a loose-based tart or cake tin, carefully lift up the tin and set it centrally on a tin of food – the side of the flan tin will drop down, leaving the tart on the metal base. If the pastry sticks to the side of the tin, just gently loosen with a table knife. Set the tart/cake on a serving plate. See page 181 for pictures of how to do this.

LUKEWARM LIQUID
Gently warm milk or water for about 20 seconds in a microwave-safe jug in the microwave or in the saucepan on the stove over very low heat. The milk or water is at the right temperature when it feels lukewarm – not hot and not cold, but ok for your finger to stay in it for 5 seconds. Ask an adult for help heating the liquid and the finger test to avoid scalding.

MELTING CHOCOLATE
Break or bash up the chocolate into small pieces and put into the heatproof bowl. Fill a saucepan one-third full of water, then bring it to the boil. Remove from the heat, then set the bowl of chocolate over the pan of steaming water, making sure the base of the bowl doesn't touch the water. Leave the chocolate to melt very gently, giving it a stir now and then. When the chocolate is smooth and melted, carefully lift the bowl off the pan and set it on a heatproof surface.

PROVING

The kneaded bread dough needs time for the yeast to do its work and produce bubbles of gas. Yeast works best in warm, moist conditions so cover the top of the bowl with clingfilm or a damp tea towel, leaving plenty of room for the dough to double in size.

The best place to leave the dough to rise or prove is on the work top – if the temperature is too warm the yeast can go crazy and the dough expand too quickly, so much that the strands of gluten that you have spent time developing during kneading snap and the dough collapses like a burst balloon.

If the temperature is really hot then the yeast – which is alive – will be killed (this is what you want to happen in the heat of the oven). You can make the yeast grow more slowly (or 'retard the dough') by leaving it to rise in an unheated room or fridge. Some recipes suggest leaving the dough in the fridge overnight so it develops in flavour as the yeast slowly grows.

ROLLING OUT

If you make your own pastry you'll need to roll it out with a rolling pin to a thin sheet before you can use it. Some biscuit doughs (like gingerbread) need rolling out as well before you cut out the shapes.

Before you start you'll need to clear and clean a space on a work top or kitchen table, then sprinkle it, your hands and the rolling pin with a little flour so the dough doesn't stick (for this reason some recipes say to chill the mixture well before you start rolling it out). Put the dough in the centre of the work top and gently press it with the rolling pin just to flatten it – sometimes you will be

asked to roll the dough to a circle or a rectangle so use your hands and the rolling pin to flatten it to a thick disc/rectangle.

Now, holding one end of the rolling pin in each hand, gently roll the pin away from you over the dough. Lift off the pin and gently neaten the sides so they keep the shape you're after, and roll again. Keep doing this, checking the dough isn't sticking to the work top by carefully lifting the edges every couple of rolls and sprinkling with a little more flour if the dough starts to stick, until you've got the dough to the thickness and/or size needed.

RUBBING IN

This is a hands-on way to combine fat - usually butter - and flour at the start of recipes for pastry (like shortcrust), scones, tray bakes, rock cakes and some other robust mixtures.

Unlike creamed mixtures, rubbed-in recipes use much less butter than flour or sugar (usually the butter is about half the weight of the flour). It's so much easier to do if the butter is cold and hard, straight from the fridge; if it is soft then the mixture turns into a greasy mess that sticks to your fingers (and goes a bit tough when it's baked). Cut the butter into tiny cubes about 0.5cm (or the size of your little finger nail) with a round-bladed knife then add them to your bowl of flour. Toss them around in the flour with the knife, so they are coated.

Now cut up the butter, in the bowl, into even tinier pieces by chopping through the mixture at random. When the mixture looks about the size of small peas, use your fingertips to reduce the butter pieces until they have become almost invisible: put both hands into the bowl and pick up a little of the butter/flour mix with your fingers only (keeping the palms of your hands clean!).

Now rub the mixture between your fingers and thumbs so the butter is squashed into the flour then drops between your fingers down into the bowl. Keep doing this for a few minutes then give the bowl a little shake – so you can spot any remaining lumps. When all the lumps of butter have disappeared and the mixture looks a bowl of crumbs (sometimes a recipe may say 'coarse crumbs', or 'fine crumbs' – which means another minute of rubbing in) it's ready for the next stage (see pages 92 and 171 for pictures of how to do this).

SEPARATING EGGS

Some recipes ask you to 'separate the eggs' – this means cracking them open and putting the yolks in one bowl and the whites in another. To separate an egg, have two bowls ready, one for the yolk and another for the white. Gently crack the egg against the rim of the bowl, then hold it over one bowl and push your thumbs into the crack to separate the two halves of the shell. Pull the shell slightly apart so the white runs into the bowl, then tip both halves upright so the yolk falls into the bottom half. Lift off the top shell so more white can drop into the bowl then tip the yolk into the empty half-shell, then back into the other half until all the white has dropped into the bowl. Tip the yolk into the second bowl. Pick out pieces of shell that have fallen into the bowl (if any specks of yellow yolk have also fallen in, carefully remove them using the empty half shell).

SKEWER TEST

Put on oven gloves, then take the bake out of the oven and set it on a heatproof surface. Push a cocktail stick into the middle of cake. If the stick comes out clean, the cake is cooked; if it comes out with sticky mix on it, put the cake back into the oven to bake for 5 minutes, then test it again. See page 24 for photos.

SIFTING

This means using a sieve to tip flour, cocoa or icing sugar into the bowl, adding air and removing any lumps at the same time. Gently tap the sieve with the side of your hand to knock the contents into the bowl.

SOFT PEAKS & STIFF PEAKS

Recipes often ask for egg whites or cream to be whisked with an electric hand held whisk to 'soft peak' stage. This means until the liquid (whites or cream) have thickened up and massively increased in volume.

It's the texture you're checking for – lift the whisk out of the mixture and look at the spot where it was. If the mixture is thick enough to have been lifted into a little peak that flops over at the tip then the mixture is at soft peak stage.

After a little more whisking the mixture will thicken and stiffen up so that when the whisk is lifted it leaves behind a peak that stands up straight and stiff and doesn't flop over. When whisking egg whites to 'stiff peak stage' it should be possible to hold the bowl upside down without the whites falling out! Try it if you dare!

See page 118 for photos of soft and stiff peaks.

SPOON MEASURES – LEVEL AND ROUNDED

All spoon measures should be flat and level unless it says otherwise. To get a level spoon measure, use a knife to scrape off the excess. Some recipes might call for 'rounded' or 'heaped' spoon measures.

AT ROOM TEMPERATURE

If a recipe calls for eggs or butter 'at room temperature', don't forget to take the butter and eggs out of the fridge at least an hour in advance. If the ingredients are too cold, it will affect the finished bake.

WHISKING

Whisking is another name for whipping. You need a whisk – either a balloon hand whisk or a hand-held electric whisk and a large bowl.

Cream, whole eggs (with or without sugar) and egg whites are the ingredients most likely to be whisked – and whisking changes them from runny liquids to firm structures that you can spread or pipe or shape.

So what happens? As you start to use the whisk, turning it around and around in the bowl, it draws air into the liquid, and millions of tiny air bubbles become trapped in the structure so at first it looks frothy then it expands enormously (and turns whiter) and looks thick and puffy.

Whole eggs and egg whites work best when they are at room temperature, so remove from the fridge about an hour before. Whites need a spotlessly clean and grease-free bowl to reach their maximum volumes, so inspect it first.

Adding a pinch of salt or cream of tartar (which is slightly acidic) will help the structure build when whisking whites for meringues. Cream works best when it's very cold and taken straight from the fridge - and in very hot weather chill the bowl and whisk in the fridge too for an hour. If you stand the bowl on a damp cloth it will stop it wobbling.

WHISKING TO RIBBON

To test if the mixture has been whisked enough lift out the whisk. If you can write your initials in the bowl with the ribbon-trail of mixture that falls off the whisk, the mixture is ready. This is known as whisking to the ribbon stage.

WORK

This is a way of saying mix or stir or blend or combine ingredients with a spoon or your hands for several seconds or minutes until they have come together or look smooth or soft or thickened – according to the recipe.

ZESTING

Zesting just means grating the rind from citrus fruits. Rinse and dry the fruit then, using a fine-hole grater, remove just the coloured rind (this is the zest). Take care to leave the white pith on the lemon because it tastes bitter.

SOME USEFUL TIPS

* Read the recipe through before you start and check that you have everything you need.
* Baking is kitchen chemistry; so you need to be accurate to be successful. Take time to carefully weigh out or measure the ingredients; use proper calibrated measuring spoons and a measuring jug rather than a spoon or jug from the cupboard.
* Measure liquids in a jug with your eye level with the surface of the liquid.
* The temperature of your oven is crucial to the success of your bake – a few degrees out either way won't hurt a casserole, but your biscuits could be toast. If you want to be sure your thermostat is accurate, buy an inexpensive oven thermometer.
* Always preheat the oven. If you put your cake mixture into a too-cool or unheated oven you'll end up with a cake only your dog will fancy.
* Keep a clean, slightly damp cloth near so you can wipe your hands when they get sticky – it'll save time cleaning up.
* Keep a spare pack of butter in the freezer just for baking emergencies, but remember to allow time for it to defrost or soften depending on your recipe. Eggs and milk are best kept in the fridge.

A BIT OF HEALTH AND SAFETY

Two things cannot be more important when cooking – keeping everything clean and keeping yourself safe from cuts, burns and scalds. Always check with an adult before you start baking – talk about what you intend to do and how you'll do it and ask for help when using sharp knives, electrical equipment and hot ovens and hobs.
* Before you start, give your hands a really good scrub with plenty of soap (and use a nailbrush for any deeply dirty nails).
* Tie back long hair so it can't get in the way, remove dangly jewellery (ditto), pull up long sleeves. You might want to wear an apron to protect your clothes because baking can get messy.
* Give the work surface a good wipe down with a clean damp cloth so it is spotlessly clean. Make sure you do the washing up with hot soapy water (rinsing off the suds) – but use cold water when you're making flour doughs for the initial clean-up or you'll have a gluey mess.
* Chopping boards need a good scrub after use (or run through the dishwasher). Take particular care if you're using meat, chicken or fish – don't use the same equipment again until it (and your hands) have been properly cleaned.
* Oven gloves are essential – do not bake without them. Always put oven gloves on when you are using the oven and stand back when you open the door so you avoid the first rush of very hot air escaping.
* Never, ever use damp oven gloves or cloths to lift tins and trays in or out of the oven.

CONVERSION TABLES

WEIGHT

Metric	Imperial		Metric	Imperial		Metric	Imperial
50g	2oz		250g	9oz		650g	1lb 7oz
75g	2½oz		300g	11oz		700g	1lb 9oz
100g	4oz		350g	12oz		750g	1lb 10oz
125g	4½oz		400g	14oz		800g	1lb 12oz
150g	5oz		450g	1lb		850g	1lb 14oz
175g	6oz		500g	1lb 2oz		900g	2lb
200g	7oz		550g	1lb 4oz		950g	2lb 2oz
225g	8oz		600g	1lb 5oz		1kg	2lb 4oz

SPOON MEASURES

Metric	Imperial
5ml	1tsp
10ml	2tsp
15ml	1tbsp
30ml	2tbsp
45ml	3tbsp
60ml	4tbsp
75ml	5tbsp

VOLUME

Metric	Imperial		Metric	Imperial		Metric	Imperial		Metric	Imperial
30ml	1fl oz		150ml	¼ pint		300ml	½ pint		500ml	18fl oz
50ml	2fl oz		175ml	6fl oz		350ml	12fl oz		600ml	1 pint
75ml	2½fl oz		200ml	7fl oz		400ml	14fl oz		700ml	1 ¼ pints
100ml	3½fl oz		225ml	8fl oz		425ml	¾ pint		850ml	1 ½ pints
125ml	4fl oz		250ml	9fl oz		450ml	16fl oz		1 litre	1 ¾ pints

 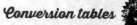

As you whisk, beat, cream or mix, use a plastic scraper to scrape down the sides of the mixing bowl every minute or so. That way all the ingredients will be evenly beaten – and there'll be no lumps!

 Take a ruler to your cake tin. If your tin is too small, the cake batter could overflow in the oven, but if your tin is too big, the cake could end up overbaked, thin and dry.

 It's also worth spending a bit of time coating the tin with a bit of butter and then lining it with baking paper – if you don't, you may end up digging your cake out of the tin.

 A digital timer with a loud beep is your friend, but don't rely on it – test the cake with a skewer or your finger – this chapter will tell you how.

 Just-baked cakes can be very fragile – handle them gently until they cool down and firm up.

 Wait until cakes are 100% cold before decorating or you run the risk of the icing slipping off.

Makes 1 medium cake
STICKY LEMON CAKE

200g unsalted butter,
   at room temperature*, plus
   extra for greasing the tin
250g caster sugar
3 eggs, at room temperature*
2 unwaxed lemons
250g self-raising flour
½ teaspoon baking powder
100ml milk, at room temperature*

FOR THE TOPPING
100g caster sugar

YOU WILL ALSO NEED
✱ 20.5cm springclip tin or deep round cake tin ✱ baking paper ✱ kitchen scissors ✱ large bowl for mixing ✱ lemon zester or grater ✱ large sieve ✱ wooden spoon or hand-held electric mixer ✱ plastic or rubber scraper ✱ wooden cocktail sticks ✱ small bowl ✱ small sharp knife ✱ chopping board ✱ lemon squeezer ✱ small spoon ✱ wire rack

Technique
The all-in-one method

This is a very simple lemon cake soaked in a delicious lemon drizzle. It's made using the all-in-one way, where everything is added in one go and given a good beating.

1 Preheat the oven to 180°C/350°F/gas 4. Lightly grease the cake tin with a little soft butter, holding it in a scrap of baking paper.

2 Cut out a large circle of baking paper about 32cm in diameter. Press it into the tin so it completely covers the base and up the sides. Press out creases and pleats around the sides to make the lining as neat as possible.

3 Put the weighed soft butter and sugar into the bowl. Crack the eggs into the bowl (then wash your hands).

4 Rinse and dry the lemons. One at a time, hold the lemons over the mixing bowl and, using the lemon zester or the fine-hole side of the grater, grate off just the yellow rind (the zest). Take care to leave the white pith on the lemon as it tastes bitter. Save the lemons to squeeze for the topping.

5 Set the sieve over the bowl and tip the flour and baking powder into it. Sift* them into the bowl by gently shaking the sieve or tapping it with your hand. Pour in the milk.

Turn over the page

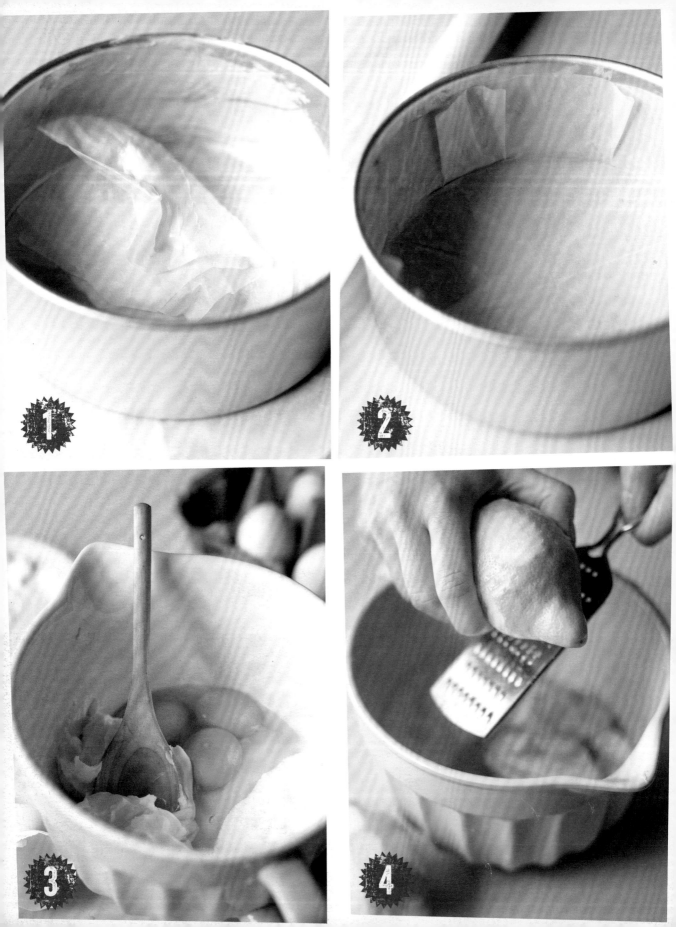

6 Set the mixing bowl on a damp towel, to prevent it from wobbling. Beat* everything together with the wooden spoon, or an electric mixer on medium speed. Scrape down the sides of the bowl every minute or so to make sure all the ingredients are mixed in.

7 Stop beating as soon as the mixture looks completely smooth, with no streaks of flour or egg.

8 Scrape the mixture into the lined cake tin and spread it out so the surface is flat. Scrape down any blobs of mixture that have splashed onto the lining paper on the sides of the tin.

9 Place in the heated oven and bake for 50–60 minutes until golden brown. To test if the cake is cooked, put on oven gloves, then take it out of the oven and set it on a heatproof surface. Push a cocktail stick into the middle of the cake*. If the stick comes out clean, the cake is cooked; if it comes out with sticky mix on it (see pic 9), put the cake back into the oven to bake for 5 more minutes, then test it again.

10 While the cake is baking, put the caster sugar for the topping into the small bowl. Cut the saved lemons in half on the chopping board, then squeeze out the juice using the lemon squeezer. Add the juice to the bowl and stir well for a minute so the sugar just starts to dissolve to make a thick syrupy mixture.

11 Wearing oven gloves, remove the cake tin from the oven and set it on the wire rack. Using a clean cocktail stick, prick the cake all over, all the way through to the tin, so it looks very holey. Quickly pour all the sugary lemon syrup over the cake. The warm cake will absorb the syrup as it cools, so don't touch it until it is cold.

12 Carefully unclip the tin side (or remove the cake from the tin). Peel off the lining paper. Set the cake on a serving platter. Store in an airtight container at room temperature. Best eaten within 4 days.

Makes 1 medium cake
BLACKBERRY CAKE

125g unsalted butter,
   at room temperature*
125g caster sugar
125g self-raising flour
1 teaspoon ground ginger
2 eggs, at room temperature*

FOR THE TOPPING
150g blackberries
75g self-raising flour
1 teaspoon ground ginger
45g caster sugar
50g unsalted butter, cold from
   the fridge, cut into 1cm cubes

YOU WILL ALSO NEED
✳ Large bowl for mixing ✳ wooden
spoon or hand-held electric mixer
✳ plastic or rubber scraper ✳ 20.5cm
springclip tin or round deep cake tin
(loose-based works best), greased
with butter and the base lined with
baking paper (page 38) ✳ colander
✳ table knife ✳ wooden cocktail stick
✳ wire rack

This quick and impressive cake uses the all-in-one method. There's a little ground ginger to add spice to the sponge and crumble topping.

1 Preheat the oven to 180°C/350°F/gas 4. Put the soft butter, sugar, flour, ground ginger and eggs into the mixing bowl. Beat* everything together with the wooden spoon or electric mixer for a minute (page 24). Scrape down the sides of the bowl, then beat for another minute or until very smooth, with no lumps or streaks. Scrape the mixture into the prepared tin and spread evenly.

2 Rinse the blackberries in the colander under the cold tap, then shake dry (or if they are quite clean, just wipe them gently with kitchen paper). Scatter them evenly over the top of the sponge mixture.

3 To make the ginger crumble topping, put the flour, ginger and sugar into the mixing bowl (no need to wash it) and mix together with your fingers. Add the butter cubes and toss them in the flour to coat, then rub in* with your fingertips until the mixture looks like small peas (page 92).

4 Scatter the crumble mixture evenly over the blackberries. Carefully place in the heated oven and bake for 50 minutes until golden brown. To test if the cake is cooked, use the skewer test* (page 24); if necessary, bake for 5 more minutes, then test again.

5 Set the tin on the wire rack and leave to cool for 5 minutes. Then loosen the sponge and remove from the tin*. Serve warm with ice cream. Or leave to cool and when cold store in an airtight container in the fridge – remove 30 minutes before serving. Eat within 3 days.

STICKY CONFETTI CAKE

125g unsalted butter,
   at room temperature*
125g caster sugar
2 eggs, at room temperature*
150g self-raising flour
1 tablespoon milk
1 teaspoon vanilla extract
5 tablespoons coloured sugar
   hundreds-and-thousands OR sugar
   strands OR coloured sweets

FOR THE ICING
250g icing sugar
100g unsalted butter,
   at room temperature*
1 tablespoon milk

YOU WILL ALSO NEED
✷ Large bowl for mixing ✷ wooden
spoon or hand-held electric mixer
✷ plastic or rubber scraper ✷ 20.5 x
25.5 x 5cm tray-bake or cake tin,
greased with butter and the base
lined with baking paper (page 38)
✷ wire rack ✷ table knife ✷ large sieve

A flat sheet of sponge can be turned into any number of different cakes – perfect for big parties and for school bake sales and fairs.

1 Preheat the oven to 180°C/350°F/gas 4. Put the soft butter and sugar into the mixing bowl. Add the eggs, flour, milk and vanilla.

2 Beat* everything together with the wooden spoon or electric mixer until very smooth and even in colour (page 24). Stop and scrape down the sides of the bowl from time to time so all the ingredients get thoroughly combined. Add 2 tablespoons of the coloured sweeties and mix them in with the scraper.

3 Scrape the mixture into the prepared tin and spread evenly, right into the corners. Place in the heated oven and bake for 20–25 minutes until the top is golden brown and the cake is starting to shrink away from the sides of the tin. To test if it's cooked, use the fingertip test*; if necessary, bake for 2–3 more minutes, then test again.

4 Set the tin on the wire rack. Loosen the cake in the tin, then leave to cool for 20 minutes. Remove from the tin*, peel off the baking paper and leave to cool completely.

5 To make the icing, sift* the icing sugar into the washed mixing bowl. Add the soft butter and milk and beat* well with the washed wooden spoon, or electric mixer on low speed, until very smooth and paler in colour. Sprinkle the remaining sweeties into the mixture and stir in.

6 Spread the icing over the top of the cold cake using the table knife. Leave to firm up in a cool spot before cutting into squares, slices or rectangles. Store in an airtight container in a cool spot (not the fridge) and eat within 4 days.

ZEBRA CAKE

225g unsalted butter,
    at room temperature*
225g caster sugar
4 eggs, at room temperature*
225g self-raising flour
½ teaspoon vanilla extract
2 ½ tablespoons milk
3 tablespoons cocoa powder

FOR THE FILLING
100g unsalted butter,
    at room temperature*
275g icing sugar
½ teaspoon vanilla extract
3 teaspoons milk
2 tablespoons cocoa powder

YOU WILL ALSO NEED
✳ Large bowl for mixing ✳ wooden
spoon or hand-held electric mixer
✳ plastic or rubber scraper ✳ medium
bowl ✳ 4 disposable piping bags
✳ 2 mugs or jugs ✳ kitchen scissors
✳ 2 x 20.5cm sandwich tins, greased
with butter and the base lined with
baking paper (page 38) ✳ wire rack
✳ large sieve

A great cake for a party – just add candles!
The sponge is a quick all-in-one mix with half
flavoured with cocoa, the other with vanilla. The
mixtures are piped in stripes into sandwich tins.

1 Preheat the oven to 180°C/350°F/gas 4. Put the soft
butter and caster sugar into the mixing bowl. Add the
eggs and flour. Beat* everything together with the
wooden spoon or electric mixer until smooth and even
in colour (page 24). Stop and scrape down the sides of
the bowl from time to time so everything is thoroughly
combined.

2 Divide the mixture in half. Scrape one portion into
the medium bowl and stir in the vanilla and 1 tablespoon
of the milk.

3 Fold down the top quarter of one of the piping bags.
Scrape the vanilla cake mixture into the bag. Unfold the
top quarter and twist the bag at the top to prevent the
mixture from escaping. Leave the bag standing in a
mug while you make up the choc mixture.

4 Add the cocoa and the remaining 1 ½ tablespoons
milk to the rest of the cake mixture and beat in well.
Fill another piping bag with this mixture.

5 Now you are ready to start piping! Snip the tip off
each bag to make an opening 2.5cm across.

6 Twist the top of the bag of white vanilla mix to force
the mixture down to the end. With one hand, hold the
bag upright over one of the prepared tins; use the other
hand to squeeze the bag and pipe a stripe of mixture
straight down the centre of the tin. Do the same thing
in the other tin.

Turn over the page

How to fill a piping bag

7 Next pipe a line of chocolate on each side of the white stripe, so the mixtures just touch. Then pipe a white stripe next to each choc stripe. Keep doing this until the tin is filled, then go back and fill in any gaps. With luck, you should get 4 stripes of each colour in each tin.

8 Place in the heated oven and bake for 20–25 minutes until the vanilla sponge stripes are golden. To test if the sponges are cooked, use the fingertip test*; if necessary, bake for a few more minutes, then test again.

9 Set the tins on a heatproof surface and cool for 5 minutes, then turn out of the tins onto the wire rack*. Peel off the lining paper and leave to cool completely.

10 Meanwhile, make the filling. Put the soft butter into the washed mixing bowl. Sift* the icing sugar into the bowl. Beat together using the washed wooden spoon, or electric mixer on low speed (to avoid a cloud of icing sugar), until very smooth and paler in colour.

11 Scrape half the filling into the washed medium bowl. Add the vanilla and 1 teaspoon of the milk and beat* until smooth and creamy. Fill a piping bag in the same way as before.

12 Sift* the cocoa into the rest of the filling, then add the remaining 2 teaspoons milk and mix well until evenly coloured and creamy. Fill the last piping bag.

13 Take a look at the 2 sponges (which are upside down on the wire rack). You want dramatic black and white stripes on top of the cake, so pick the sponge with the best-looking stripes for the top layer. Set the other sponge on a board or serving platter.

14 Snip the ends off the piping bags to make an opening 2cm across, then pipe stripes of icing over the bottom cake – in the same way as you did before. Set the other sponge gently on top. Store in an airtight container and eat within 5 days.

DOTTY CAKE

Use a medium spoon to drop alternate spoonfuls of the 2 mixtures into the tins in a random dotty pattern. Bake and cool exactly as in the main recipe. Make up both the vanilla and choc fillings and spoon in blobs rather than piping. Experiment with different edible food colourings – orange for tiger stripes or leopard spots.

Makes 6
PASSIONFRUIT CAKES

120g unsalted butter,
   at room temperature*
120g caster sugar
2 eggs, at room temperature*
120g self-raising flour
½ teaspoon baking powder
2 passionfruits

FOR THE ICING
1 passionfruit
about 75g icing sugar

YOU WILL ALSO NEED
✱ Large bowl for mixing ✱ large sieve
✱ chopping board ✱ small sharp knife
✱ small sieve ✱ small bowl or cup
✱ small spoon ✱ wooden spoon
✱ hand-held electric mixer ✱ plastic
or rubber scraper ✱ 6 card mini-loaf
cake cases, set on a baking sheet
✱ wire rack ✱ medium bowl

Fresh passionfruit juice is an easy way to turn a simple all-in-one sponge into something a bit exotic and colourful.

1 Preheat the oven to 180°C/350°F/gas 4. Put the soft butter, caster sugar and eggs into the mixing bowl. Sift* the flour and baking powder into the bowl.

2 Cut the passionfruits in half on the chopping board. Set the small sieve over the small bowl, then scoop the seeds and flesh from each half into the sieve. Press with the back of the spoon to extract all the juice. Pour the juice into the mixing bowl; throw away the black seeds.

3 Beat* everything together with the wooden spoon or electric mixer until very smooth and you can't see any streaks (page 24). Stop and scrape down the sides of the bowl every minute so everything gets mixed in.

4 Spoon the mixture into the 6 card cake cases (on the baking sheet) to fill evenly. Spread right into the corners. Carefully place in the heated oven and bake for 20–25 minutes until golden brown. To test if the cakes are cooked, use the fingertip test*; if necessary, bake for another minute, then test again. Slide the cake cases off the sheet onto the wire rack and leave to cool completely.

5 To make the icing, cut the passionfruit in half and press out the juice into the medium bowl as you did before. Sift* in the icing sugar and stir with the juice until very smooth. The icing needs to be thick enough to coat the spoon, so add a little more icing sugar if needed.

6 Drizzle the icing over the top of the cakes. Leave to set. Store in an airtight container and eat within 3 days.

CHOCOLATE SANDWICH

225g unsalted butter, at room
   temperature*, plus extra
   for greasing the tins
225g caster sugar
4 eggs, at room temperature*
200g self-raising flour
25g cocoa powder
1–2 tablespoons milk

FOR THE QUICK FUDGY ICING
75g icing sugar
20g cocoa powder
50g unsalted butter
50g caster sugar

PLUS your choice of decorations:
mini eggs, birthday candles, edible
sprinkles, mini sweets, choc flakes,
edible sugar flowers

YOU WILL ALSO NEED
✱ 2 x 20.5cm sandwich tins ✱ baking
paper ✱ pencil ✱ kitchen scissors
✱ 2 large bowls for mixing ✱ wooden
spoon or hand-held electric mixer
✱ plastic or rubber scraper
✱ small bowl ✱ fork ✱ medium spoon
✱ large sieve ✱ large metal spoon
✱ table knife ✱ wire rack ✱ small
saucepan ✱ palette knife

Technique
The creaming method

This cake is made using the 'creaming' method*. It's a great cake to know how to bake because you can then customize it for all kinds of occasions, changing the filling, topping and decorations.

1 Preheat the oven to 180°C/350°F/gas 4. Set one of the tins on a sheet of baking paper and draw around the base with the pencil. Cut out the paper circle. Do this again to cut out a second circle of paper.

2 Put a small dab of very soft butter onto a scrap of baking paper and rub it all around the inside of each tin, right up to and around the rim, so the inside of the tin is completely coated with butter (or you can spray the tins with non-stick cake spray).

3 Press a paper circle, pencil-marked side down, onto the base of each tin, smoothing out any wrinkles or air bubbles. You can use this same method to line the base of square or rectangular tins or baking sheets.

4 Put the weighed soft butter into one of the mixing bowls. Set the bowl on a damp cloth to stop it wobbling, then beat* the butter for a minute with a wooden spoon or electric mixer until very smooth and creamy-looking.

5 Add the sugar and beat for a minute. Scrape down the sides of the bowl so all the mixture gets evenly mixed using the scraper. Beat for another minute, then scrape down again. Do this 2 more times or until the mixture looks paler in colour and fluffier in texture because of the air you've beaten into it (this is creaming*). The creaming will take 4–5 minutes using the wooden spoon or about 3 minutes with the mixer.

6 Crack the eggs into a small bowl (wash your hands)*, then beat* together with the fork for a few seconds, just to break up the yolks and mix them with the whites.

Turn over the page

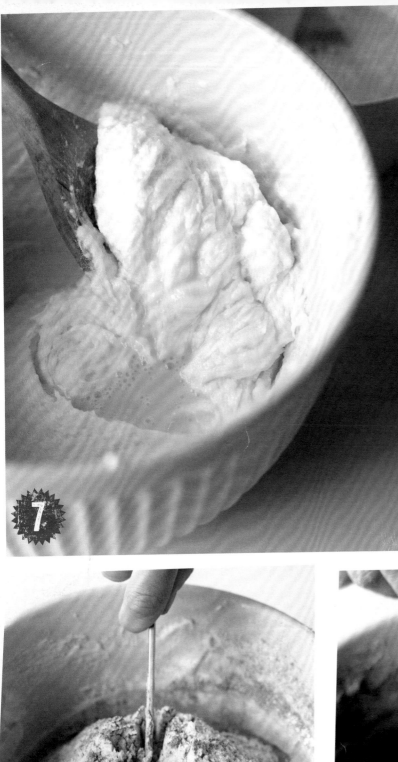

7 Add a spoonful of the eggs to the butter mixture and beat* for 20 seconds until it disappears into the mixture. Keep adding the eggs to the mixture, a spoonful at a time and beating well after each is added. Stop every minute or so to scrape down the sides of the bowl (and to rest if you're using a wooden spoon for beating).

8 When only a couple of tablespoons of egg are left in the small bowl, add a tablespoon of the weighed flour to the mixing bowl. Mix the flour into the beaten mixture, a tablespoon at a time, followed by a tablespoon of egg and beat well. Add the last portion of egg and briefly beat it in just until it disappears. Adding flour now will help prevent the mixture from curdling. Don't worry if your mixture does look a bit curdled – your cake will taste just fine although it may not rise quite as high. The beating stage will take about 5 minutes so don't try to rush it.

9 Set the sieve over the bowl. Tip the rest of the flour and the cocoa powder into it, then sift* the flour and cocoa into the bowl.

10 Add 1 tablespoon milk to the bowl. Now use the large metal spoon to fold* everything together. To begin, use the side of the spoon to cut down through the centre of the mixture until the spoon hits the bottom of the bowl. Turn the spoon to scoop and lift up some of the mixture from the bottom and gently flip it over onto the top.

11 Rotate the bowl a little, so you can start in a different place, then cut down again with the spoon, lift up and flop (or fold) the mixture over. Keep rotating the bowl, cutting and flopping until you can't see any specks or streaks of flour or cocoa and everything looks smooth and evenly coloured. The mixture should have a 'dropping consistency' – it should fall easily from the spoon when you shake it. If the mixture is too stiff or heavy to do this, fold in another tablespoon of milk.

Turn over the page

12

13

14

15

16

12 Spoon the mixture into the tins, dividing it equally – check by eye or by weighing (this is easy if you have digital scales). Gently spread the mixture right to the edges of the tins. Carefully place the tins in the heated oven and bake for 20–25 minutes. To test if the sponges are cooked, put on oven gloves, then carefully lift the tins out of the oven and set them on a heatproof surface. Use the finger test to check if the cakes are cooked*.

13 Set the tins on the heatproof surface. Loosen the sponges in the tins, then leave them to cool and firm up for a couple of minutes. Place the wire rack next to the tins. Wearing oven gloves, turn out the loosened sponges*. Peel the baking paper off the sponges. Leave them to cool completely.

14 To make the fudgy icing, sift* the icing sugar and cocoa powder into the other mixing bowl. Put the butter, caster sugar and 2 tablespoons water into the saucepan and set it over low heat. Stir gently with the washed wooden spoon until the butter has completely melted and the grains of sugar have disappeared so the mixture no longer feels gritty when you stir. Turn up the heat. When the mixture starts to boil, with big bubbles breaking over the surface, immediately turn off the heat.

15 Carefully pour the hot mixture into the mixing bowl and stir to mix with the icing sugar. Once everything is evenly mixed, beat* well with the wooden spoon for a minute to make the icing smooth and glossy. Leave it to cool and become firm enough to spread.

16 Set one sponge cake on a serving plate. Spread over half of the fudgy icing using the palette knife. Set the other sponge on top, crust side up. Dollop the rest of the icing on top and gently swirl it over the sponge. Add your decorations, then leave to set before cutting. Store in an airtight container and eat within 4 days.

SUMMER CHOCOLATE CAKE

Once cooled, spread the bottom sponge layer with 4 tablespoons strawberry jam. Whip 125ml cold whipping cream and spread on top. Remove the green stalks and leaves from 200g small ripe strawberries and arrange them on top of the cream. Gently set the second sponge on top and finish with sifted* icing sugar. Store in an airtight container in the fridge and eat within 2 days.

HOT CHOC CAKE

200g dark chocolate (with 70% cocoa solids for the best taste)*, broken into pieces

125g unsalted butter, cut into small pieces

5 large eggs, at room temperature, whites and yolks separated* into the 2 mixing bowls

125g caster sugar

50g plain flour

icing sugar, for dusting

YOU WILL ALSO NEED

✴ Heatproof bowl ✴ table knife ✴ medium saucepan ✴ wooden spoon ✴ 2 large bowls for mixing ✴ electric mixer ✴ large metal spoon ✴ plastic or rubber scraper ✴ 20.5cm springclip cake tin, greased with butter and the base lined with baking paper (page 38) ✴ wooden cocktail stick ✴ wire rack ✴ small sieve or tea strainer

A really rich cake made with plenty of chocolate. It's best served while still very slightly warm from the oven, but it's good the next day too. Serve with ice cream to turn it into a dessert.

1 Preheat the oven to 180°C/350°F/gas 4. Gently melt the chocolate* in a saucepan with the butter until smooth. Leave to cool.

2 Using the electric mixer, whisk the egg whites until they stand up in stiff peaks* (page 119). Put the bowl to one side.

3 Add the sugar to the egg yolks and beat* with the electric mixer (there's no need to wash it) until the mixture is very thick and pale in colour, and is at the 'ribbon stage'*.

4 Sprinkle the flour over the egg yolk mixture. With the edge of the large metal spoon, fold in the flour (page 40).

5 Scrape the chocolate mixture into the yolk mixture and fold in*. Add a third of the whisked egg whites to the bowl and gently fold in. Fold in the remaining egg whites in 2 more batches.

6 Spoon the mixture into the tin and spread evenly. Place in the heated oven and bake for 30 minutes. To test if the cake is cooked, use the skewer test* – the cocktail stick should come out with a bit of mixture stuck to it as the cake will be slightly gooey in the middle (page 24).

7 Set the tin on the wire rack and leave to cool until the cake is just warm, then unclip the side of the tin and remove it*. Set the cake on a serving platter, sprinkle lightly with sifted* icing sugar and serve.

BANANA LOAF

100g unsalted butter
250g self-raising flour
150g light brown muscovado sugar
2 large eggs, at room temperature*
250g peeled ripe bananas (2–3)
3 tablespoons cocoa powder
3 tablespoons hot water from
   the kettle
icing sugar and cocoa powder,
   for dusting

YOU WILL ALSO NEED
✱ Small saucepan ✱ 2 large bowls
for mixing ✱ wooden spoon ✱ fork
✱ small heatproof bowl ✱ plastic
or rubber scraper ✱ several small
spoons ✱ 9 individual card loaf cases,
set on a baking sheet ✱ wire rack
✱ small sieve or tea strainer

MAKE IT LARGE

Make the same mixture. Grease
a 900g loaf tin (about 26 x 12.5 x
7.5cm) with butter and line with a
long strip of baking paper (page
38). Fill the tin with the 2 mixtures
as in the main recipe, but using
pairs of medium spoons (the sort
you eat with). Swirl to marble the
mixtures. Bake for about 45
minutes; test using the skewer
test* (page 24). Set the tin on a
wire rack and cool completely
before removing from the tin*.

A chocolate muffin-banana bread combination
that's perfect for a quick treat. The card cases
are great for protecting the loaves in a lunchbox
or for packing for a picnic.

1 Preheat the oven to 180°C/350°F/gas 4. Put the butter
in the saucepan and melt gently over low heat; cool. Put
the flour and sugar into one of the mixing bowls and stir
with the wooden spoon to break up any lumps of sugar.

2 Add the eggs to the pan of cool but still melted butter
and mix well with the fork. Use the fork to mash the
bananas on a plate – there should still be some small
lumps. Add the egg mixture and the bananas to the
flour mixture and mix well with the wooden spoon.
Spoon half of the mixture into the other mixing bowl.

3 Put the cocoa into the heatproof bowl and carefully
stir in the hot water to make a smooth paste. Stir the
cocoa paste into one portion of the banana mixture.

4 Using 2 small spoons for each mixture (one for
scooping the mix and the other for scraping it off the
spoon), add alternate spoonfuls of the banana mix and
cocoa mix to the loaf cases – you'll need 3 teaspoons of
each mixture for each case. You can leave them looking
like dark and light spots, or swirl the 2 colours together
by drawing a chopstick or spoon handle through them.

5 Place in the heated oven and bake the loaves for
20–25 minutes. To test if they are cooked, use the
fingertip test*; if necessary, bake for 5 more minutes,
then test again. Wearing oven gloves, lift the little
cases onto the wire rack and leave to cool. Before
serving, sprinkle lightly with sifted* icing sugar and
then with cocoa powder.

Makes 1 medium cake
SIMPLE SWISS ROLL

3 eggs, at room temperature*
75g caster sugar, plus extra
   for sprinkling
75g plain flour

FOR THE FILLING
2 medium Bramley cooking apples
2–3 tablespoons caster sugar, to taste
3 tablespoons Greek-style yoghurt

YOU WILL ALSO NEED
✳ Large bowl for mixing ✳ hand-held
electric mixer ✳ large sieve ✳ large
metal spoon ✳ plastic or rubber
scraper ✳ swiss roll or baking tin
20 x 30cm, greased with butter and
the base lined with baking paper
(page 38) ✳ baking paper ✳ large
sharp knife ✳ wire rack ✳ vegetable
peeler✳ chopping board ✳ small
sharp knife✳ medium saucepan ✳
wooden spoon✳ medium spoon

This is a classic cake – a very light, rolled-up
sponge. The mixture is made by whisking eggs
and sugar together to trap millions of tiny air
bubbles – these are what make the sponge rise.

1 Preheat the oven to 220°C/425°F/gas 7. Break the
eggs into the mixing bowl and whisk* with the electric
mixer on high speed for a few seconds until the yolks
have broken up and the eggs look a bit frothy.

2 Add the sugar and whisk*, still on high speed, for
about 5 minutes until the mixture becomes much paler
in colour and really thick and fluffy. It is whisked enough
when it has reached the 'ribbon stage'*.

3 Sift* the flour onto the foamy egg mixture. With the
edge of the large metal spoon, fold* the mixture until
you can't see any streaks of flour (page 40).

4 Carefully scrape the delicate mixture into the
prepared tin and gently spread it into the corners.
Place in the heated oven and bake for 9–10 minutes
until the sponge is golden brown. To test if it is cooked,
use the fingertip test*; if necessary, bake for another
minute, then test again.

5 Lay a sheet of baking paper about 30 x 40cm on the
worktop. Sprinkle it with a little caster sugar. Wearing
oven gloves, turn the tin over on the sugared paper and
shake gently to remove the cooked sponge, then lift off
the tin. Peel off the baking paper.

Turn over the page

How to roll a sponge

6 With the large sharp knife, make a shallow cut along one short end of the sponge, about 2cm in from the edge. (This will help give the roll a neat spiral when it is sliced.) Starting from the end with the cut, gently roll up the warm sponge with the paper inside (so the paper is rolled up too). Set the roll on the wire rack and leave it until cold.

7 To make the filling, peel the apples with the vegetable peeler, then set them on the chopping board. Cut them into quarters. Cut away the cores, then cut each quarter into 4 or 5 thick slices.

8 Put the apples into the saucepan with 4 tablespoons water. Set the pan over medium-low heat and cook, stirring every minute or so with the wooden spoon, until the apples feel soft and start to break up when prodded with the spoon. Turn up the heat to medium and cook, stirring constantly, for a couple of minutes until you can no longer see any liquid and the mixture is thick and jam-like rather than runny. Carefully remove from the heat and leave to cool.

9 Add 2 tablespoons sugar and the yoghurt to the cold apples and stir to mix well. Taste the mixture and add a little more sugar if it isn't sweet enough.

10 Carefully unroll the sponge. Spoon the apple mixture over the surface and spread evenly. Gently re-roll the sponge from the end with the cut (it will now have a 'memory' and rolling should be easy). Be sure you leave the paper on the worktop. Sprinkle with a little more sugar and serve as soon as possible. The roll can be kept, tightly covered, in the fridge for up to 24 hours – take out an hour before serving.

STRAWBERRY & CREAM ROLL

Spread 6 tablespoons strawberry jam over the sponge. Whip* 200ml whipping cream in a mixing bowl using a hand-held electric mixer until thick. Spread on top of the jam, then roll up the sponge. Serve as soon as possible.

PEACHY UPSIDE-DOWN CAKE

FOR THE TOPPING
3 medium peaches
2 tablespoons light brown
  muscovado sugar

FOR THE GINGERBREAD
100ml milk, at room temperature*
1 egg, at room temperature*
50g unsalted butter
50g light brown muscovado sugar
50g black treacle
50g golden syrup
125g self-raising flour
½ teaspoon bicarbonate of soda
½ teaspoon ground cinnamon
1 ½ teaspoons ground ginger

YOU WILL ALSO NEED
✱ Chopping board ✱ small sharp
knife ✱ medium bowl ✱ medium
spoon ✱ small saucepan ✱ wooden
spoon ✱ large sieve ✱ large bowl
for mixing ✱ measuring jug ✱ fork
✱ plastic or rubber scraper ✱ 20.5cm
springclip tin or round deep cake tin,
greased with butter and the base
lined with baking paper (page 38)

A good bake for a wet afternoon in summer
when peaches are plentiful (choose fruit that
is fairly firm rather than soft and ripe). At
other times of year you can use well-drained
tinned peaches.

1 Preheat the oven to 180°C/350°F/gas 4. Rinse the
peaches and pat dry with kitchen paper. Set them on
the chopping board. One at a time, slice in half with the
small knife, then twist gently to loosen the stone and
pull the halves apart. If you can, pull out the stone now.
Cut each half in half, then remove the stone if it's still
there. Cut the quarters into large chunks – about 3cm.

2 Put the peach chunks into the medium bowl. Sprinkle
over the 2 tablespoons sugar and stir gently so the
peaches are coated in sugar. Leave until needed.

3 Now make the gingerbread mixture. Put the butter,
sugar, black treacle and golden syrup into the saucepan.
Set it over very low heat and stir gently with the wooden
spoon until the butter has melted and the mixture is
smooth. Carefully remove from the heat and leave to
cool until needed.

4 Set the large sieve over the mixing bowl and tip the
flour into the sieve. Add the bicarbonate of soda, ground
cinnamon and ginger. Sift* these dry ingredients into
the bowl.

5 Pour the milk into the measuring jug. Crack the
egg into the jug*. Beat* with the fork for a few seconds
to break up the egg and mix everything together.

6 Scrape the melted mixture from the saucepan into the bowl with the flour. Pour in the milk mixture. Set the bowl on a damp cloth to stop it wobbling, then beat* everything together with the wooden spoon to make a thick, sticky, smooth mixture.

7 Spoon the peaches into the prepared tin, leaving any juices behind in the bowl, and spread them out evenly. Scrape the gingerbread mixture into the tin to cover the peaches.

8 Place in the oven and bake for about 35 minutes. To test if the cake is cooked, put on oven gloves and do the fingertip test*. If the sponge feels soft and soggy return it to the oven to bake for 2 more minutes, then test again.

9 Loosen the sponge in the tin*. Now you will need the help of an adult. Turn a large serving platter with a rim upside down and set it on top of the tin. Wearing oven gloves, hold the plate and tin firmly together, then quickly turn them together over so the cake flops out onto the plate. Leave to cool until just warm before serving with ice cream, or eat cold. Best the same day.

Makes 8
LITTLE MAPLE CAKES

125g unsalted butter,
  at room temperature*
50g light brown muscovado sugar
150ml maple syrup
2 large eggs, at room temperature,
  lightly beaten*
125g self-raising flour
100g pecan halves

FOR THE TOPPING
5 tablespoons maple syrup
150g cream cheese

YOU WILL ALSO NEED
✷ Large bowl for mixing ✷ 1 small
bowl ✷ fork ✷ wooden spoon ✷ 8 card
mini-loaf cases, set on a baking sheet
✷ fish slice ✷ wire rack ✷ small spoon
✷ small baking sheet or dish, lined
with baking paper ✷ table knife

Maple syrup and pecans are a great combination, and they make an all-in-one sponge mix into something special. The maple topping just takes a couple of minutes and each cake is finished with a candied pecan.

1 Preheat the oven to 180°C/350°F/gas 4. Put the soft butter, sugar and maple syrup into the mixing bowl. Add the eggs and flour to the bowl. Mix* everything together with the wooden spoon.

2 Pick out 8 good-looking pecan halves and set aside for the decoration. Break the rest into 2 or 3 pieces with your hands. Add to the cake mixture and stir in. Spoon the mixture into the card loaf cases so they are evenly filled.

3 Place in the heated oven and bake for 25–30 minutes. To test if the cakes are cooked, use the fingertip test*. With the fish slice, transfer the cases to the wire rack and leave to cool completely, but do not turn the oven off.

4 Put the 8 reserved pecans into a small bowl with a tablespoon of the maple syrup and mix well. Spoon onto the small baking sheet or dish, arranging the nuts close together in one layer. Place in the oven and bake for 10 minutes until the syrup is bubbling. Wearing oven gloves, remove the sheet and set it on a heatproof surface. Leave until cold.

5 Put the cream cheese and remaining 4 tablespoons maple syrup in the washed mixing bowl and beat* with the washed wooden spoon until creamy and smooth.

6 Spread the sweet cream cheese topping over the cold cakes and decorate each with a candied pecan.

BIG RASPBERRY CAKE

250g unsalted butter,
  at room temperature*
250g caster sugar
4 eggs, at room temperature,
  lightly beaten*
250g self-raising flour
75g ground almonds
225g fresh raspberries
  (ripe but firm, not soft)
icing sugar, for sprinkling

YOU WILL ALSO NEED
✳ Large bowl for mixing ✳ wooden
spoon or hand-held electric mixer
✳ plastic or rubber scraper ✳ small
bowl ✳ fork ✳ medium spoon ✳ large
sieve ✳ large metal spoon ✳ 20.5cm
springclip tin or deep round cake tin,
greased with butter and the base
lined with baking paper (page 38)
✳ wooden cocktail stick ✳ wire rack
✳ small sieve or tea strainer

BLUEBERRIES

Use fresh blueberries instead
of raspberries and add the finely
grated zest (the yellow rind)
of an unwaxed lemon* to the
butter with the sugar.

When fresh raspberries are at their mid-summer finest, make this huge sponge cake to eat after a barbecue, with scoops of ice cream.

1 Preheat the oven to 180°C/350°F/gas 4. Put the butter into the mixing bowl and beat* with the wooden spoon or electric mixer for a minute until the butter is smooth and creamy (page 38). Add the sugar and beat until pale and fluffy. Scrape down the sides of the bowl from time to time.

2 Gradually add the eggs, beating* in each addition until it disappears before adding the next. Scrape the bowl every minute or so. When you are left with just a couple of tablespoons of egg, beat a tablespoon of flour into the mixture between each addition of egg.

3 Sift* the rest of the flour onto the mixture. Sprinkle the ground almonds on top. With the edge of the large metal spoon, gently fold* in the ground almonds until you can't see any streaks of flour (page 40).

4 Scatter half the raspberries over the mixture and gently fold in*. Scrape the mixture into the prepared tin and spread evenly, right to the edges. Scatter the rest of the raspberries on top – they will slowly sink in.

5 Carefully place in the heated oven and bake for 1–1 ¼ hours until the cake is golden brown. To test if the cake is cooked, use the skewer test* (page 24); if necessary, bake for 5 more minutes, then test again.

6 Set on the wire rack and leave to cool before removing from the tin*. Sift icing sugar over the top of the cake. Store in an airtight container in a cool place or the fridge (take out 30 minutes before serving). Eat within 3 days.

Cuts into 20 pieces
SQUIDGY BROWNIES

200g unsalted butter
100g bar dark chocolate
200g caster sugar
4 eggs, at room temperature*
½ teaspoon vanilla essence
75g plain flour
25g cocoa powder
100g your choice of extras: walnut
   or pecan pieces OR white, dark
   or milk choc chips

YOU WILL ALSO NEED
✳ Table knife ✳ small heavy-based
saucepan ✳ rolling pin ✳ wooden
spoon ✳ large bowl for mixing ✳ wire
whisk or electric mixer ✳ plastic or
rubber scraper ✳ large sieve ✳ 20.5
x 30.5cm traybake tin or cake tin
✳ greased with butter and the base
lined with baking paper (page 38)
✳ wooden cocktail stick ✳ wire rack.

Technique
The melting method

Really good brownies are irresistible, and
these have melted chocolate and cocoa for a
fudgy flavour and texture. You can add your
own extras – nuts, or even more chocolate.
This recipe uses the melting method, also used
in the making of gingerbread and flapjacks.

1 Preheat the oven to 180°C/350°F/gas 4. Cut the butter
into sticks and put in the saucepan. Use the rolling pin
to bash up the bar of chocolate (still in its wrapper) on
the worktop, then tip the pieces into the saucepan.

2 Set the pan on the lowest possible heat and leave
the butter and chocolate to melt gently, stirring every
minute or so with the wooden spoon. Take the pan off
the heat as soon as the mixture is smooth, so it doesn't
become too hot. Leave the pan on a heatproof surface
until needed.

3 Put the sugar and eggs into the mixing bowl. Beat*
with the wire whisk or electric mixer for 2 minutes until
thoroughly combined and the mixture is slightly frothy.

4 Pour the melted chocolate into the bowl and whisk it
in for a minute until you can no longer see any streaks
of dark brown.

5 Sift* the flour and cocoa into the bowl. Stir into the
chocolate mixture with the wooden spoon (there's no
need to wash it).

Turn over the page

6 When everything is combined, stir in your choice of extras, distributing them evenly.

7 Scrape the mixture into the prepared tin and spread it out, making sure it goes right into the corners. Gently bang the tin on the worktop to knock out pockets of air.

8 Carefully place in the heated oven and bake for 20 minutes. To test if the brownie is cooked, use the skewer test* (page 24); if necessary, bake for 2 more minutes and test again.

9 Wearing oven gloves, set the tin on the wire rack and leave to cool before cutting into squares. Store in an airtight container and eat within 5 days.

PEANUT BUTTER BROWNIES

Make up the mixture but don't stir in any extras. Instead, mix together 175g smooth peanut butter (use the no-added-sugar type if possible), 1 tablespoon plain flour, 5 tablespoons milk and 40g caster sugar. Transfer the chocolate brownie mixture to the tin and spread it evenly. Drop small spoonfuls of the peanut mixture onto the chocolate mixture (make sure the blobs are evenly spaced). Then swirl the 2 mixtures together with the spoon handle to give a slightly marbled effect. Bake at 180°C/350°F/gas 4 for 20 minutes or until cooked.

BONFIRE BROWNIES

FOR THE BROWNIE MIXTURE
125g unsalted butter,
    at room temperature*
175g light brown muscovado sugar
3 large eggs, at room temperature,
    lightly beaten*
100g plain flour
30g cocoa powder
1 teaspoon vanilla extract (optional)
100g pecan pieces or choc chips
    (optional)

TO FINISH
100g mini marshmallows
100g unsalted butter
40g cocoa powder
3 tablespoons milk
300g icing sugar

YOU WILL ALSO NEED
✴ Large bowl for mixing ✴ wooden
spoon or hand-held electric mixer
✴ plastic or rubber scraper ✴ small
bowl ✴ fork ✴ large metal spoon
✴ traybake tin, cake tin or roasting
tin about 25.5 x 20.5 x 5cm, greased
with butter and the base lined with
baking paper (page 38) ✴ saucepan
✴ table knife

A dark, soft brownie with hidden depths, topped with melted marshmallows and fudge frosting – very gooey and very good for sharing.

1 Preheat the oven to 200°C/400°F/gas 6. Put the soft butter and sugar into the mixing bowl and beat* together with the wooden spoon or electric mixer until creamy, smooth and fluffy (this is creaming, page 38). Stop and scrape down the sides of the bowl once or twice.

2 Add the eggs to the creamed mixture a little at a time, beating well after each addition and scraping down the sides of the bowl from time to time (page 38).

3 Add the flour, cocoa and vanilla extract, if using. Gently fold* in using the large metal spoon (page 38). Stir in the nuts or choc chips, if using. When everything is thoroughly combined, scrape the mixture into the prepared tin and spread it evenly with the scraper.

4 Carefully place in the oven and bake for 15 minutes. Wearing oven gloves, remove the tin from the oven and set on a heatproof surface. The brownie mixture will be soft on top and very hot. Scatter over the marshmallows, then return to the oven and bake for a further 5 minutes until the marshmallows are starting to melt. Remove from the oven and set on a heatproof surface again.

5 Melt the butter for the icing in the saucepan over low heat. Remove from the heat. Add the cocoa, milk and icing sugar and stir thoroughly to make a thick and smooth fudgy icing.

6 Pour the warm icing over the warm brownie mixture and quickly spread over the top. Leave to cool, then cut into squares and remove from the tin. Store in an airtight container and eat within 4 days.

Learn to Bake

CUPCAKES & LITTLE BAKES

Turn the oven on before you begin – these little bakes won't take much time to prepare and you don't want your batter to sit around for too long waiting for the oven to heat up.

 Get the right size – muffins and cupcakes need a larger case than fairy cakes and buns, so check the label on the pack.

 Improvise – if you don't have a muffin or cupcake tray, use 2 paper cases (one inside the other) for each bake and set them on a baking sheet.

 Don't over mix. Muffins are usually less sweet than cupcakes and are often made by quickly mixing all the ingredients; this gives them a slightly open and rough texture – too much mixing and they may become rubbery.

 They will cook quickly, but always use a cocktail stick to test for 'doneness' so you don't get a soggy centre.

 Cool the finished bakes properly. If you let them cool in the tray, the steam will condense and the bakes will go soggy. Instead carefully tip them out of the tin and put on a wire rack.

CARROT CAKE MUFFINS

75g shredded bran cereal
225ml milk
1 medium orange
120g cream cheese
1 tablespoon caster sugar
3 large carrots
125g light brown muscovado sugar
200g self-raising flour
1 teaspoon baking powder
1 ½ teaspoons ground cinnamon
1 teaspoon ground ginger
2 eggs
4 tablespoons sunflower oil

YOU WILL ALSO NEED
✶ Large bowl for mixing ✶ wooden spoon ✶ lemon zester or grater ✶ 2 small bowls ✶ chopping board ✶ small sharp knife ✶ vegetable peeler ✶ sieve ✶ fork ✶ medium-sized spoon ✶ 12-hole muffin tray, lined with paper muffin case ✶ small spoon ✶ wire rack

You can have all the same flavours and textures of carrot cake in a muffin, plus the sweet cream cheese icing as a surprise filling.

1 Put the bran cereal and milk into the mixing bowl and stir just to mix. Leave to soak for 15 minutes. Meanwhile, preheat the oven to 220°C/425°F/gas 7.

2 Rinse and dry the orange. Grate the zest from the orange into a small bowl* (page 22).

3 Tip half the zest into the large mixing bowl with the cereal and milk and put to one side. Add the cream cheese and caster sugar to the remaining zest in the small bowl and mix well – this will be your filling.

4 Put the carrots on the chopping board and, with the small sharp knife, trim off each end. Peel the carrots (you won't need the peel or trimmings).

5 Using the coarse-hole side of the grater (there's no need to wash it if you used it for the orange zest), grate the carrots onto the board. Weigh out 150g grated carrot and add to the large bowl. (You can save any leftover carrots for a salad.)

6 By now the cereal will be very mushy. Add the brown sugar to the big bowl and mix well with the wooden spoon.

Turn over the page

6

7 Set the sieve over the bowl and tip the flour, baking powder, cinnamon and ginger into it. Sift* these ingredients into the bowl by gently shaking the sieve or tapping it with your hand. Don't mix them in just yet.

8 Break the eggs into the second small bowl (then wash your hands). Add the oil to the bowl and beat* with a fork just until the egg yolks are broken up and mixed with the whites. Tip into the big bowl and mix everything together with the wooden spoon.

9 Using the medium-sized spoon, drop a dollop of the carrot mixture into each paper muffin case in the tray. Drop a small spoonful of the cream cheese filling into the middle.

10 Then cover the filling with the rest of the carrot mixture, dividing it evenly among the cases. Place in the heated oven and bake for about 20 minutes until golden brown. Check the muffins are cooked by using the fingertip test*.

11 Wearing oven gloves, remove the tray from the oven and set it on a heatproof surface. Leave for 5 minutes, then carefully transfer the muffins to the wire rack to cool. Store in an airtight container and eat within 24 hours.

BERRY-LEMON MUFFINS

60g unsalted butter,
   at room temperature*
150g caster sugar
1 unwaxed lemon
2 eggs, at room temperature,
   lightly beaten*
275g self-raising flour
½ teaspoon bicarbonate of soda
125ml natural yoghurt
200g fresh blueberries

YOU WILL ALSO NEED

✳ Large bowl for mixing ✳ lemon zester or grater ✳ wooden spoon or hand-held electric mixer ✳ small bowl ✳ fork ✳ medium-sized spoon ✳ large sieve ✳ small sharp knife ✳ lemon squeezer ✳ small spoon ✳ 12-hole muffin tray, lined with paper muffin cases ✳ wooden cocktail stick ✳ wire rack

These are slightly sweet and bursting with fruit – perfect for popping into a lunchbox.

1 Preheat the oven to 200°C/400°F/gas 6. Put the soft butter and sugar into the bowl. Grate the zest from the lemon into the bowl* (page 22); save the lemon for later. Beat the butter with the sugar and zest using the wooden spoon or electric mixer for a couple of minutes until creamy, smooth and fluffy (this is creaming*, page 38).

2 Add a spoonful of beaten egg and beat well for a minute, then add another spoonful and beat again. Keep adding the beaten egg like this until it's all added. Don't worry if the mixture looks a bit sloppy. Sift* the flour and bicarbonate of soda into the bowl.

3 Cut the lemon in half, then squeeze the juice from one half. Measure 1 tablespoon of juice and stir it into the yoghurt. Pour the yoghurt mixture into the bowl. Gently stir everything together with the wooden spoon. Tip the blueberries into the bowl and gently mix in.

4 Spoon the mixture into the paper muffin cases in the tray, making sure there is the same amount in each – it's easiest if you use a small spoon for this.

5 Place in the heated oven and bake for 20–25 minutes until golden brown. To test if the muffins are cooked, use the skewer test* on a muffin in the centre of the tray; if necessary, bake for 2 more minutes (page 24).

6 Wearing oven gloves, remove the tray from the oven and set it on a heatproof surface. Leave for 5 minutes before transferring the muffins to the wire rack to cool. Store in an airtight container and eat within 24 hours.

RASPBERRY AND GRANOLA MUFFINS

250g plain wholemeal flour
½ teaspoon ground cinnamon
1 teaspoon baking powder
½ teaspoon bicarbonate of soda
200g light brown muscovado sugar
100g crunchy granola
250g natural low-fat yoghurt
100ml milk
75ml sunflower oil
150g fresh raspberries

FOR THE TOPPING
75g crunchy granola

YOU WILL ALSO NEED
✻ Large bowl for mixing ✻ wooden
spoon ✻ medium-sized spoon
✻ 12-hole muffin tray, lined with
paper muffin cases ✻ wooden
cocktail stick ✻ wire rack

Good for breakfast, these moist and fruity muffins are speedy to put together. Use your favourite granola to add crunch.

1 Preheat the oven to 200°C/400°F/gas 6. Put the flour, cinnamon, baking powder, bicarbonate of soda, sugar and granola into the mixing bowl. Stir together with the wooden spoon, then make a well in the centre of the mixture.

2 Pour the yoghurt, milk and oil into the well and stir everything together. Add the raspberries and mix in gently.

3 Using the medium-sized spoon, drop the mixture into the paper muffin cases in the muffin tray, making sure you put an equal amount in each. Sprinkle the top of each muffin with a little granola.

4 Place the tray in the heated oven and bake for about 25 minutes until golden brown. To test if the muffins are cooked, use the skewer test* on a muffin in the centre of the tray; if necessary, bake for 2 more minutes, then test again (page 24).

5 Wearing oven gloves, remove the tray from the oven and set it on a heatproof surface. Leave for 5 minutes, then carefully transfer the muffins to the wire rack to cool. These are best eaten the same day.

XMAS PUDS

100g unsalted butter
2 tablespoons black treacle
2 tablespoons golden syrup
100g dark brown muscovado sugar
100ml milk
175g plain flour
1 teaspoon bicarbonate of soda
1 tablespoon ground ginger
1 teaspoon ground cinnamon
1 egg, at room temperature,
  lightly beaten*
50g chocolate chips (the ones with
  about 54% cocoa solids work best)

TO FINISH
100g icing sugar
edible decorations, such as sugar
  holly leaves or glacé cherries
  (optional)

YOU WILL ALSO NEED
✱ Medium saucepan ✱ wooden
spoon ✱ sieve ✱ large bowl for mixing
✱ small bowl ✱ fork ✱ medium-sized
spoon ✱ 12-hole muffin tray, lined
with 9 paper muffin cases ✱ wooden
cocktail stick ✱ wire rack ✱ small
spoon ✱ small bowl

Sticky, spicy gingerbread and chocolate muffins that look like xmas puds when iced. Go as festive as you like with the decoration.

1 Preheat the oven to 190°C/375°F/gas 5. Put the butter, treacle, golden syrup, sugar and milk in the saucepan. Set it over low heat and warm gently, stirring now and then with the wooden spoon, until the butter has melted and the sugar has dissolved. Remove from the heat and leave the mixture to cool for 10 minutes.

2 Meanwhile, sift* the flour, bicarbonate of soda, ginger and cinnamon into the mixing bowl. Tip the cooled melted mixture into the mixing bowl and add the egg. Stir well with the wooden spoon until smooth and thick but still runny. Stir in the chocolate chips.

3 Spoon the mixture into the 9 paper cases to fill evenly. Place in the heated oven and bake for 15–20 minutes until well risen. To test if the muffins are cooked, use the skewer test* on a muffin in the centre of the tray; if necessary, bake for 2 more minutes, then test again (page 24).

4 Wearing oven gloves, remove the tray from the oven and set it on a heatproof surface. Cool for 5 minutes, then carefully transfer the muffins to the wire rack and leave to cool completely.

5 Mix the icing sugar with 2 teaspoons cold water to make a thick but spreadable icing. Dollop a small spoonful of icing onto the centre of each muffin, then use the back of the spoon to spread the icing over the top. Add decorations before the icing sets. Once the icing has set firm, store the muffins in an airtight container and eat within 3 days.

HALLOWE'EN CUPCAKES

100g unsalted butter, at room
   temperature*
100g caster sugar
2 eggs, at room temperature*
1 small orange
100g self-raising flour

TO FINISH

3 tablespoons fine-shred or jelly
   marmalade
icing sugar for dusting
6 glacé cherries or round jelly sweets
450g pack ready-to-roll white sugar
   paste icing
12 currants

YOU WILL ALSO NEED

✳ Large bowl for mixing ✳ lemon
zester or grater ✳ small sharp knife
✳ lemon squeezer ✳ wooden spoon or
hand-held electric mixer ✳ medium-
sized spoon ✳ 6-hole muffin tray lined
with paper muffin or cupcake cases
✳ wooden cocktail stick ✳ wire rack
✳ small saucepan ✳ pastry brush
✳ rolling pin ✳ small plate or saucer
15cm across ✳ table knife

These fun ghosts are really orange-flavoured cupcakes with cherries or jelly sweets for heads plus ready-to-roll white icing for the ghostly covering. For extra spookiness, why not spray your ghosts with edible shimmer spray?

1 Preheat the oven to 190°C/375°F/gas 5. Put the soft butter and sugar into the mixing bowl. Add the eggs.

2 Grate the zest from the orange* (page 22). Cut the orange in half and squeeze the juice from one half. Measure 2 teaspoons of juice into the mixing bowl (save the rest to add to a drink or fruit salad). Add the flour to the bowl, then mix everything together very well with the wooden spoon or electric mixer.

3 Spoon the mixture into the 6 paper cases in the muffin tray so they are evenly filled. Place the tray in the heated oven and bake for 20–25 minutes until golden brown and well risen. To test if the muffins are cooked, use the skewer test* on a muffin that's in the centre of the tray; if necessary, bake for 2 more minutes, then test again (page 24).

4 Wearing oven gloves, remove the tray from the oven and set it on a heatproof surface to cool for 5 minutes. Transfer the cupcakes to the wire rack and leave to cool.

Turn over the page

5 When you're ready to decorate the cupcakes, put the marmalade in the saucepan and warm gently over low heat until melted.

6 Peel off the paper cases and set the cupcakes upside down on a serving plate or board. Use the pastry brush to coat the flat top and sides of the cupcakes with warm marmalade. Stick a cherry or round jelly sweet on top of each cupcake, dead centre, for the ghost's head.

7 Lightly sprinkle the worktop with icing sugar, then roll out* the white icing to a large rectangle slightly thinner than a pound coin. Using the saucer or plate as a guide, cut out circles of icing with the table knife. Knead* the icing scraps into a ball, then roll out and cut more circles until you have 6.

8 Drape a circle of white icing over each cupcake so it looks like a sheet-covered 'ghost'. Press 2 currant 'eyes' on each ghost. Store the cupcakes in an airtight container and eat within 2 days.

Makes 12
CHOC-TOFFEE CUPCAKES

175g self-raising flour
25g cocoa powder
175g light brown muscovado sugar
100g unsalted butter, at room
   temperature*
2 eggs, at room temperature*
125ml milk, at room temperature*
12 soft chocolate-covered toffees
   (e.g. Rolos)

YOU WILL ALSO NEED
✶ Sieve ✶ large bowl for mixing
✶ wooden spoon or hand-held
electric mixer ✶ plastic or rubber
scraper ✶ small spoon ✶ 12-hole
muffin tray, lined with paper muffin
or cupcake cases ✶ wire rack

An all-in-one mixture is used here to make
chocolate cupcakes with a chocolate-toffee
centre.

1 Preheat the oven to 180°C/350°F/gas 4. Sift* the flour,
cocoa powder and sugar into the mixing bowl. Add the
soft butter and eggs. Pour in the milk. Beat* together
with the wooden spoon or electric mixer to make a
smooth, thick mixture. Scrape down the sides of the
bowl from time to time to be sure everything is mixed in.

2 Spoon a little of the mixture (a heaped small spoonful)
into each paper case, then put a toffee in the middle.
Cover with more cake mixture, spooning an equal
amount into each paper case so they are evenly filled.

3 Place the tray in the heated oven and bake for about
20 minutes. To test if the cupcakes are cooked, use the
fingertip test*. Wearing oven gloves, remove the tray
from the oven and set on a heatproof surface.

4 Leave to cool for 2 minutes, then carefully transfer the
cupcakes to the wire rack and leave to cool completely.
Store in an airtight container and eat within 4 days.

VANILLA CUPCAKES

175g unsalted butter, at room
   temperature*
3 eggs, at room temperature*
100ml milk, at room temperature*
250g caster sugar
250g self-raising flour
1 teaspoon vanilla extract

QUICK VANILLA ICING

75g unsalted butter, at room
   temperature*
250g icing sugar
1 teaspoon vanilla extract
4 tablespoons milk
coloured sprinkles, to decorate

YOU WILL ALSO NEED

✱ Large bowl for mixing ✱ wooden
spoon or hand-held electric mixer
✱ plastic or rubber scraper ✱ medium
spoon ✱ 12-hole muffin tray, lined
with paper muffin or cupcake cases
✱ wooden cocktail stick ✱ wire rack
✱ small bowl ✱ table knife

Home-made cakes always taste the best, even
if you are only using them as the base for some
very creative icing and decorating. There are
some icing ideas below – from very quick to
rich and fudgy.

1 Preheat the oven to 180°C/350°F/gas 4. Put all the
cupcake ingredients into the mixing bowl and beat well
with the wooden spoon or electric mixer for a couple
of minutes until creamy, smooth and fluffy* (page 24).
Don't forget to scrape down the sides of the bowl a few
times so all the ingredients are thoroughly combined.

2 Spoon the mixture into the paper cases in the muffin
tray, making sure they are evenly filled.

3 Place in the heated oven and bake for 25–30 minutes
until the cupcakes are well risen and golden brown.
To test if they are cooked, use the skewer test* on a
muffin that's in the centre of the tray; if necessary, bake
for 2 more minutes, then test again (page 24).

4 Wearing oven gloves, remove the tray from the oven
and set it on a heatproof surface. Cool for 2 minutes,
then transfer the cupcakes to the wire rack and leave
until completely cold before icing. Store in an airtight
container and eat within 4 days.

5 To make the icing, put the butter in the small bowl
with the icing sugar, vanilla extract and milk. Beat*
with the wooden spoon, or hand-held electric mixer on
low speed, for about 3 minutes until creamy and light.
Spread or swirl onto the cupcakes with the table knife.

Turn over the page

RASPBERRY CUPCAKES

Set a fresh raspberry on the top of each cupcake before putting the tray in the oven to bake. Make the Quick Vanilla Icing (page 80), adding 60g raspberries to the icing ingredients instead of the milk. Beat well so the berries colour and flavour the icing evenly.

CHOCOLATE FUDGE TOPPING

Bash up a 100g bar dark chocolate and put into a small heatproof bowl. Add 1 tablespoon golden syrup and 25g unsalted butter. Pour some water into a small pan so it is about a third full, then bring it to the boil. Turn off the heat and carefully set the bowl over the pan. Stir gently with a wooden spoon until everything is smooth and melted. Carefully lift the bowl off the pan and set it on a heatproof surface. Leave to cool for about 5 minutes until the mixture is thick enough to spread, then use the table knife to swirl it over the top of the cupcakes. If you fancy it, add sprinkles or chocolates or chunks of honeycomb (see page 128). Leave to set.

CHEESY CORN MUFFINS

These slightly spicy, savoury muffins are quick to make when you need something tasty for a picnic, or to go with soup.

1 Preheat the oven to 200°C/400°F/gas 6. Put the milk and butter in the saucepan and warm over a low heat until the butter has melted. Leave to cool for 5 minutes.

2 Meanwhile, grate the cheese onto a plate, using the coarse-hole side of the grater. Add the paprika and cayenne and toss with the cheese. Tip three-quarters into the mixing bowl; save the rest for the topping. Add the flour and frozen sweetcorn to the mixing bowl and mix well with the cheese.

3 Crack the eggs into the cooled milk mixture (then wash your hands). Mix with the fork for a few seconds, then pour into the big bowl. Stir with the wooden spoon until everything has come together to make a slightly rough-looking mixture. Spoon the mixture into the paper cases in the muffin tray, making sure there is the same amount in each case. Sprinkle the saved grated cheese on top.

4 Place the tray in the heated oven and bake for about 25 minutes until well risen and golden brown. To test if the muffins are cooked, use the skewer test* on a muffin that's in the centre of the tray; if necessary, bake for 2 more minutes, then test again (page 24).

5 Wearing oven gloves, remove the tray from the oven and set it on a heatproof surface. Leave for a couple of minutes before transferring the muffins to the wire rack. Eat warm or at room temperature. Once cold, store in an airtight container and eat the same or the next day.

350ml milk
100g unsalted butter
175g Gruyère, Emmental or
   Cheddar cheese
½ teaspoon sweet smoked paprika
¼ teaspoon cayenne pepper
500g self-raising flour
150g frozen sweetcorn
2 eggs, at room temperature,
   lightly beaten*

YOU WILL ALSO NEED

✱ Small saucepan ✱ grater ✱ plate ✱ large bowl for mixing ✱ wooden spoon ✱ fork ✱ medium-sized spoon ✱ 12-hole muffin tray, lined with paper muffin or cupcake cases ✱ wooden cocktail stick ✱ wire rack

MEATY MUFFINS

Add some spicy diced chorizo, or cooked bacon, to the mixture (no more than 75g) before you add the eggs.

Makes 8
TOAD IN THE HOLE

115g plain flour
good pinch of black pepper
2 eggs, at room temperature
275ml milk
3 tablespoons rapeseed
   or vegetable oil
8 chipolata sausages

YOU WILL ALSO NEED
✳ Large bowl for mixing ✳ wire
whisk ✳ small spoon ✳ 2 x 4-hole
non-stick Yorkshire pudding tins
✳ large measuring jug ✳ table knife

The all-time great combination of sausages baked in Yorkshire pudding. Just pick your favourite thin sausages, whisk up the batter and you're ready to go. You can make the same batter, and cook it in the same way, minus the sausages, when you want Yorkshires to go with a roast.

1 Put the flour and pepper in the mixing bowl. Crack the eggs into the bowl (wash your hands after you do this)*, then pour in the milk. Use the whisk to mix the whole lot together until you can't see any lumps. Leave this batter to rest for 30 minutes – the resting time will make it rise a bit better during baking.

2 Preheat the oven to 220°C/425°F/gas 7. Spoon a little oil into each hole of the Yorkshire tins, then set a sausage in the middle – you may have to curve it gently to fit. Put the tins into the oven and bake for 5 minutes.

3 Meanwhile, whisk the batter for a couple of seconds to make sure it is smooth, then pour it into the measuring jug. Wearing oven gloves, remove the tins from the oven and set them on a heatproof surface. The fat in the tin will be very hot so take extra special care. Pour batter into each hole, filling it almost but not quite to the top.

4 Carefully return the tins to the oven and bake for 20–25 minutes until the batter is golden brown and looks crisp. Wearing oven gloves, remove the tins from the oven and set on the heatproof surface. With the help of the table knife, gently ease each toad out of the tin. Eat straight away.

Makes 4
VEGGIE FRITTATA

2 spring onions
1 courgette (about 150g)
1 red pepper
8 cherry tomatoes
2 tablespoons rapeseed or olive oil
good pinch each of dried chilli
   flakes and black pepper
130g ball mozzarella
4 eggs
6 tablespoons double or single cream

YOU WILL ALSO NEED
✱ Chopping board ✱ small sharp
knife ✱ kitchen scissors (optional)
✱ non-stick frying pan ✱ wooden
spoon ✱ large jug ✱ fork ✱ non-stick
4-hole Yorkshire pudding tin,
greased with butter ✱ medium
spoon ✱ table knife

The perfect Mother's Day lunch. This is a kind of baked omelette, Italian style, packed with vegetables and stringy melted mozzarella. Try it with salad or a baked potato.

1 Preheat the oven to 190°C/375°F/gas 5. Lay the spring onions on the chopping board and very carefully trim off the hairy root ends using the small sharp knife or scissors, then cut off the dark leafy tops at the other end. Rinse the trimmed spring onions under the cold tap and shake dry. Put them back on the chopping board and slice across into thinnish rounds. Push them to one side of the board.

2 With the small knife, slice off each end of the courgette, then rinse it under the tap. Put the courgette back on the board and slice it lengthways in half. Set each half flat side down on the board, so they won't slip. Cut each half lengthways in half again so you now have 4 long strips. Cut across the strips to make 1cm chunks. Push them over with the onions.

3 Rinse the pepper, then lay it on its side on the board and cut off the green stalk end. Turn the pepper so it is standing on the cut end and carefully cut it in half lengthways. Pull out the core with all the seeds from each half, and pull out or trim off the white 'ribs'. Cut the pepper flesh into strips the thickness of your little finger, then cut across the strips into 1cm chunks. Rinse the tomatoes, then put them on the board and slice lengthways in half.

Turn over the page

Turn over the page

4 Spoon the oil into the non-stick frying pan and set it on the stove over low heat. When the oil is hot, carefully add all the vegetables, plus the chilli flakes and black pepper. Stir well with the wooden spoon. Turn up the heat to medium and fry, stirring carefully every minute, for 7–10 minutes until the courgettes are speckled with golden brown spots. Wearing oven gloves, take the pan off the heat and leave the mixture to cool.

5 Tear or cut up the mozzarella into chunks about 2cm in size. Break the eggs into the jug (wash your hands after you do this) and pour in the cream. Whisk together for a few seconds with the fork until well mixed.

6 Set the frying pan on a heatproof surface next to the buttered Yorkshire tin. Spoon the vegetable mixture into the middle of each hole so it is piled up. Put the cheese on top. Pour the egg mix into each hole to fill it.

7 Very carefully transfer the tin to the heated oven and bake for about 25 minutes until puffed and a good golden brown. Wearing oven gloves, remove the tin from the oven and set it on a heatproof surface. Gently remove the frittatas from the tin, using the table knife to help you, and place on serving plates. Eat at once.

A FLORAL FINISH

For a special touch, decorate the plates with edible flowers, such as English daisies, pansies, nasturtiums and violets, as well as sprigs of fresh herbs.

SIMPLE SCONES

250g self-raising flour
50g caster sugar
50g unsalted butter,
    cold from the fridge
3 tablespoons natural yoghurt
milk
1 egg, lightly beaten*

YOU WILL ALSO NEED
✳ Large bowl for mixing ✳ table knife
✳ small bowl ✳ fork ✳ measuring jug
✳ 6cm round cutter ✳ baking sheet,
lightly rubbed with butter ✳ wire rack

Technique
The rubbing-in method

Scones may be as old as the hills but they are still a treat eaten warm with good jam and thick cream. Any leftover scones are good split in half and toasted.

1 Preheat the oven to 220°C/425°F/gas 7. Tip the flour and sugar into the mixing bowl. Cut the butter into small cubes about the size of your thumbnail and add to the bowl. Use the knife to toss the pieces of butter in the flour so all are coated.

2 Rub the flour and butter together with your fingertips until the mixture looks like small pieces of rubble (this is called rubbing in). While you're rubbing in, lift your hands up just above the rim of the bowl so the mixture falls through your fingers.

3 Spoon the yoghurt into the measuring jug and pour in enough milk to measure 100ml. Add the beaten egg and mix together with the fork. Pour the egg mixture into the mixing bowl. Mix into the crumbs, first with the table knife and then, as soon as the mixture starts to stick together, with your hands.

4 Gather the dough to make a slightly soft ball. Sprinkle a little flour over the worktop, then turn out the ball of dough onto it. Gently press and squeeze the dough together for a couple of seconds just to bring it together neatly.

Turn over the page

5 Sprinkle your hands with a little flour, then pat out the dough about 3cm thick. Dip the cutter in flour and cut out rounds of dough. Set them, about 2cm apart, on the buttered baking sheet. Press the dough scraps together and pat out again, then cut more rounds to make 8 in total.

6 Place in the heated oven and bake for 12–15 minutes until golden brown. Wearing oven gloves, remove the sheet from the oven and set it on a heatproof surface. Transfer the scones to the wire rack and leave to cool slightly before serving warm. These are best eaten the same day.

APPLE SCONES

Add 1 large tart dessert apple (quartered, cored and cut into 1cm chunks) to the mixture at the end of step one.

CHEESY SCONES

Leave out the sugar and add ½ teaspoon mustard powder and 50g grated strong Cheddar to the mixture at the end of step one, then sprinkle the scones with 25g grated cheese just before they go into the oven.

CHORIZO SCONES

Leave out the sugar and add 50g sweet smokey paprika chorizo (use a pack of thin sliced, and cut each slice into 4 with kitchen scissors) to the mixture at the end of step one.

Learn to Bake

BISCUITS

This is the best place to start if you've never baked before!

 You will need one good baking sheet. Pick one that fits your oven and is of fairly good quality – 'bargain' sheets can buckle in the heat of the oven and scorch your efforts.

 Leave space between your biscuits on the sheet – most recipes spread out as they bake, so if you don't leave enough space, you could end up with one big cookie.

 Aim to make the biscuits or cookies an even size so they cook at the same pace. If some are thinner than others, they will cook faster and even burn before the others are done.

 If you need to bake in several batches, don't put the second batch of biscuit dough straight onto a hot baking sheet as the dough will melt and spread out. Hold (with oven gloves) the sheet under the cold tap for a few seconds. Dry then re-use.

 Use the wire rack from the grill pan if you don't have a cooling rack.

CHOC CHIP SANDWICHES

125g unsalted butter, at room
   temperature*
200g light brown muscovado sugar
1 egg, lightly beaten*
220g plain flour
3 tablespoons cocoa powder
¾ teaspoon baking powder
PLUS 200g of your choice of extras:
   white, milk OR dark choc chips
   OR chunks and walnut, pecan
   OR brazil nut pieces

YOU WILL ALSO NEED
✷ Large bowl for mixing ✷ wooden
spoon or hand-held electric mixer
✷ plastic or rubber scraper
✷ small bowl ✷ fork ✷ sieve
✷ 2–3 baking sheets, lined with
baking paper (if you only have
one baking sheet, you can bake
the cookies in batches, see page 95)

For the ultimate treat, sandwich two of these chocolatey cookies with a scoop of ice cream.

1 Preheat the oven to 180°C/350°F/gas 4. Put the soft butter and sugar into the mixing bowl and beat with the wooden spoon or electric mixer until the mixture looks creamy, smooth and fluffy (this is creaming, see page 38)*. Scrape down the sides of the bowl from time to time so everything gets thoroughly beaten.

2 Add the egg to the mixing bowl and beat* very well, scraping down the sides of the bowl every now and then. Sift* the flour, cocoa and baking powder into the bowl and mix in with the wooden spoon. When uniformly chocolate brown with no streaks, tip in your chosen extras and mix into the cookie dough with the wooden spoon or your hands until evenly distributed.

3 Dip your hands in cold water and shake off the drops, then shape the dough into pingpong-sized balls (if the dough gets sticky, dip your hands in water again). Set the balls, spaced well apart, on the lined baking sheets.

4 Place in the heated oven and bake for 15 minutes until slightly darker around the edges. Wearing oven gloves, remove the sheets and set them on a heatproof surface. Leave to cool completely before removing the cookies from the sheets. Store in an airtight container and eat within 5 days.

Makes about 18
LEMON FORKIES

250g unsalted butter,
    at room temperature*
65g icing sugar
1 medium unwaxed lemon
75g cornflour
225g plain flour

YOU WILL ALSO NEED
✷ Large bowl for mixing ✷ wooden
spoon or hand-held electric mixer
✷ lemon zester or grater ✷ 2 baking
sheets, lined with baking paper (if
you only have one baking sheet, you
can bake the cookies in batches,
see page 95) ✷ fork ✷ wire rack

Buttery, melt-in-the-mouth biscuits that take
no time at all to make – once the ingredients are
mixed you get your hands into the bowl to make
pingpong sized balls, which get squashed with
a fork and baked. That's it!

1 Preheat the oven to 180°C/350°F/gas 4. Put the soft
butter and icing sugar into the large mixing bowl. Grate
the zest from the lemon into the bowl*. Beat* with the
wooden spoon or electric mixer for a couple of minutes
until the mixture looks creamy, smooth and fluffy (this
is creaming*, page 38). Add the cornflour and flour to
the bowl and stir in with the wooden spoon.

2 When everything is completely mixed together, use
your hands to roll the dough into pingpong-sized balls
(if the mixture feels very sticky sprinkle a little flour on
your hands). Set the balls on the lined baking sheets,
spacing them about 5cm apart to allow for spreading
during baking.

3 Dip a fork in flour, then gently press a pattern onto
each ball – you can make a noughts and crosses grid,
a starburst or plain lines.

4 Place in the heated oven and bake for 15–20 minutes
until the edges are just turning golden. Wearing oven
gloves, remove the sheets from the oven and set them
on the wire rack. Leave the biscuits to cool completely.
Store in an airtight tin and eat within 4 days.

CRUNCHY CHEWY OATIES

100g unsalted butter,
    at room temperature*
100g light brown muscovado sugar
50g caster sugar
1 teaspoon ground cinnamon
1 egg
85g plain flour
½ teaspoon baking powder
150g porridge oats
100g jumbo raisins OR dried
    cherries OR dried cranberries
    OR walnut pieces

YOU WILL ALSO NEED
✳ Large bowl for mixing ✳ wooden
spoon or hand-held electric mixer
✳ plastic or rubber scraper ✳ medium
spoon ✳ 1–2 baking sheets, lined with
baking paper (if you only have one
baking sheet, you can bake the
cookies in batches, see page 95)
✳ wire rack

Crunchy and chewy and a little spicy –
everything you want from an oat cookie.
If you're not a fan of raisins you can add
other dried fruits or nuts.

1 Preheat the oven to 180°C/350°F/gas 4. Put the soft
butter, both sugars and the cinnamon into the mixing
bowl. Beat well with the wooden spoon or electric mixer
for about 2 minutes until the mixture looks creamy,
smooth and fluffy (this is creaming).

2 Break the egg into the bowl (wash your hands) and
beat again for a couple of minutes. Scrape down the
sides of the bowl now and then so all the ingredients
get smoothly mixed together.

3 Add the flour and baking powder to the bowl and mix
in with the wooden spoon. Add the oats and the raisins
(or whatever you want to add) and mix well.

4 Use the medium-sized spoon to drop the mixture in
craggy 5cm balls onto the lined baking sheets – make
sure you space them at least 5cm apart to allow for
spreading during baking.

5 Place in the heated oven and bake for 15 minutes
until golden. Wearing oven gloves, remove the sheets
from the oven and set them on the wire rack. Leave
the biscuits to cool before lifting them off the sheets.
Store in an airtight container and eat within 5 days.

DAD'S CHEESY BISCUITS

125g plain wholemeal flour
85g unsalted butter, cold from
  the fridge
85g extra-mature Cheddar cheese,
  coarsely grated
½ teaspoon Worcestershire sauce

YOU WILL ALSO NEED
✳ Grater ✳ large bowl for mixing
✳ table knife ✳ clingfilm ✳ chopping
board ✳ large sharp knife ✳ baking
sheet, lined with baking paper

A tasty snack for dads and granddads, these savoury biscuits are really easy to make and are the perfect Father's Day or Christmas treat (but you can eat them too!).

1 Put the flour into the mixing bowl. Using the table knife, cut the butter into small pieces – about the size of your thumbnail – and add to the flour. Mix together with your hands until the butter pieces are coated with flour.

2 Rub the mixture between your fingertips, letting it fall back into the bowl (this is rubbing in*, page 92). Continue doing this, making sure you gather up all the flour and butter at the bottom of the bowl, until the mixture looks like pieces of gravel.

3 Add the grated cheese and Worcestershire sauce. Put your hands into the bowl and gently press and squeeze everything together until it is thoroughly combined.

4 Tip the mixture out onto a worktop. Shape into a log 10cm long and 6cm across. Wrap it in clingfilm. Chill in the fridge for an hour (the tightly wrapped dough can be kept in the fridge for 24 hours). Towards the end of the chilling time, preheat the oven to 180°C/350°F/gas 4.

Turn over the page

Rolling and shaping
your biscuits

5 Unwrap the dough and set it on the chopping board. Carefully cut the dough log across into 12 even slices using the large sharp knife. Lay the slices on the lined baking sheet. Make sure they are about 5cm apart in case they spread during baking.

6 Place in the heated oven and bake for 15–18 minutes until the biscuits are turning golden brown around the edges. Wearing oven gloves, remove the baking sheet from the oven and set it on a heatproof surface. Leave until the biscuits are cold before lifting them off the baking sheet. Store in an airtight container and eat within 4 days.

CHEESE-TASTIC

Try using flavoured Cheddar, or, if your dad likes blue cheese, try using Stilton instead.

Makes 16
SUNSHINE FLAPJACKS

75g ready-to-eat dried apricots
115g unsalted butter, plus extra
   for greasing
70g light brown muscovado sugar
5 tablespoons golden syrup
180g porridge oats
75g mixed seeds

YOU WILL ALSO NEED
✳ Kitchen scissors ✳ large saucepan
✳ wooden spoon ✳ 20.5cm square tin,
greased with butter ✳ wire rack
✳ table knife.

GOLDEN SYRUP

Don't be tempted to add more
golden syrup – your cooked
flapjack will go rock hard
when cold!

These are sticky and chewy flapjacks packed
with good stuff. You can add seeds from a
mixed pack, or a combination of your favourites
like sunflower, pumpkin and sesame seeds.

1 Preheat the oven to 150°C/300°F/gas 2. Use the
scissors to snip the apricots into small pieces the
size of your thumbnail.

2 Put the butter, sugar and golden syrup into the
saucepan (it needs to be large enough to hold all the
ingredients). Set it on top of the stove over low heat and
stir with the wooden spoon until the butter has melted.

3 Take the pan off the heat and set it on a heatproof
surface. Add the oats, seeds and apricots to the pan
and stir the mixture well.

4 When everything is thoroughly combined, scrape
the mixture into the greased tin. Spread it evenly, right
into the corners, then lightly press the mixture down
with the back of the spoon so the surface is level.

5 Place in the heated oven and bake for 20 minutes
until the edges are turning golden brown. Wearing
oven gloves, remove the tin from the oven and set
it on the wire rack.

6 Rub the table knife with a little butter to grease it, then
carefully score the hot flapjack mixture into 16 squares.
Leave until cold before removing the squares from the
tin. Store in an airtight container and eat within a week.

Makes about 30
VANILLA STARS

250g unsalted butter,
   at room temperature*
125g caster sugar
1 teaspoon vanilla extract
1 egg, white and yolk separated*
   into 2 bowls
300g plain flour, plus extra
   for rolling out
100g dark chocolate, for dipping
edible sprinkles, to decorate

YOU WILL ALSO NEED
✻ Large bowl for mixing ✻ wooden
spoon or hand-held electric mixer
✻ small bowl ✻ clingfilm ✻ rolling pin
✻ 7.5cm star cutter ✻ 2 baking sheets,
lined with baking paper (if you only
have one baking sheet, you can bake
the cookies in batches, see page 95)
✻ wire rack

You can use this mixture to make crisp
biscuits in other shapes, using biscuit cutters
or by cutting around cardboard cut-outs.

1 Put the soft butter, sugar and vanilla into the mixing
bowl and beat with the wooden spoon or electric mixer
for about 2 minutes until creamy, smooth and fluffy*
(page 38).

2 You don't need the egg white for this recipe, so keep
it, covered, in the fridge for another use. Add the egg
yolk to the butter mixture and beat* for a minute. Add
the flour and mix in with the wooden spoon at first and
then with your hands to make a ball of dough.

3 Divide the dough in half and shape each piece into
a flat disc about 3cm thick. Wrap in clingfilm and chill
for about an hour until firm. Towards the end of this
time preheat the oven to 180°C/350°F/gas 4.

4 Sprinkle a little flour on the worktop. Unwrap one
piece of dough and roll out* with the rolling pin until
slightly thicker than a pound coin. Dip the cutter in flour
and cut out star shapes. Arrange them about 3cm apart
on the lined baking sheets. Gather up the scraps into
a ball, then roll out as before and cut out more shapes.
Repeat with the other piece of dough.

5 Place in the heated oven and bake for 10–15 minutes
until light golden and the edges are just turning light
brown. Wearing oven gloves, remove the sheets from the
oven and set them on the wire rack. Leave the biscuits
until they are completely cold, then lift them off the paper.

6 Gently melt the chocolate* and then carefully dip each
cooled biscuit into the chocolate. Before the chocolate
sets, sprinkle the biscuits with edible decorations.
Store in an airtight container and eat within 5 days.

Makes about 16
EASTER BISCUITS

125g unsalted butter,
   at room temperature*

75g caster sugar

1 medium unwaxed lemon

1 egg, white and yolk separated*
   into 2 bowls

200g plain flour, plus extra
   for rolling out

¼ teaspoon baking powder

50g dried sour cherries,
   sultanas or raisins

coloured caster sugar, for sprinkling

YOU WILL ALSO NEED

✶ Large bowl for mixing ✶ wooden
spoon or hand-held electric mixer
✶ lemon zester or grater ✶ small bowl
✶ rolling pin ✶ 6.5cm round fluted or
other shaped cookie cutter ✶ table
knife ✶ 2 baking sheets, lined with
baking paper (if you only have one
baking sheet, you can bake the
cookies in batches, see page 95)
✶ fork ✶ pastry brush

KEEP IT NATURAL

Look for coloured sugars made
using natural dyes and always
check the labels of edible food
colourings before using.

Colourful lemon-flavoured biscuits with a
crunchy coating – why not experiment with
cutter shapes and colours.

1 Preheat the oven to 200°C/400°F/gas 6. Put the soft
butter and sugar into a mixing bowl and beat* well for
a minute with the wooden spoon or electric mixer.

2 Grate the zest from the lemon* into the bowl (page
22). Beat well for another minute until the mixture looks
very creamy, smooth and fluffy (this is creaming).

3 Add the egg yolk, then beat the mixture for another
minute. Save the egg white – you'll need it later.

4 Add the flour, baking powder and dried fruit to the
bowl and mix in with the wooden spoon. As soon as the
mixture becomes too stiff to mix with the spoon, put
your hands into the bowl and squash the mixture into
a ball. Make sure the fruit has been evenly mixed in
and is not all in one spot.

5 Sprinkle a little flour on the worktop, then tip out the
dough onto it. Rub a little flour onto the rolling pin and
roll out the dough until it is thickness of two stacked up
pound coins*. Dip the cutter in flour and cut out rounds
or other shapes – press down hard so you cut through
the fruit (dip the cutter in flour again if it starts to stick).

6 Lift the shapes with your fingers onto the lined baking
sheets, keeping the shapes about 5cm apart (they may
spread during baking). If bits of fruit fall off as you
transfer the shapes, just push them back together.
Gather up all the dough scraps left on the worktop and
press into a ball, then roll out as you did before and cut
out more shapes. Set them on the sheets too.

Turn over the page

7 Place in the heated oven and bake for about 10 minutes until pale gold. Wearing oven gloves, remove the sheets from the oven and set on a heatproof surface.

8 Beat the saved egg white with the fork for a few seconds until frothy, then lightly brush each biscuit with it, using the pastry brush. Sprinkle over a little coloured sugar. Wearing oven gloves, return the sheets to the oven and bake for 3 more minutes.

9 Remove from the oven, set the baking sheets on the heatproof surface and leave to cool completely. When the biscuits are cold, lift them off and store in an airtight tin for up to 4 days.

Makes 8 pairs
CORNFLAKE KISSES

100g unsalted butter, at room
    temperature*
70g caster sugar
1/2 teaspoon vanilla extract
1 large egg, at room temperature,
    white and yolk separated*
    into 2 bowls
about 25g cornflakes (regular
    or chocolate-flavoured)
150g self-raising flour
about 3 tablespoons jam and/
    or peanut butter, or chocolate
    spread, for sandwiching

YOU WILL ALSO NEED
✳ 2 small bowls or cups ✳ large
bowl for mixing ✳ wooden spoon
or hand-held electric mixer
✳ plastic or rubber scraper ✳ dinner
plate ✳ 2–3 baking sheets, lined with
baking paper (if you only have one
baking sheet, you can bake the
cookies in batches, see page 95)
✳ wire rack ✳ table knife

Sandwich these crunchy bites with jam,
peanut butter or chocolate spread.

1 Preheat the oven to 190°C/375°F/gas 5. Put the soft
butter into the mixing bowl with the sugar and vanilla
and beat with the wooden spoon or electric mixer until
creamy, smooth and fluffy* (page 38). Scrape down the
sides of the bowl so all the mixture is beaten in.

2 You only need the egg yolk, so save the egg white for
another recipe. Add the egg yolk to the mixing bowl and
beat* well for 2 minutes, scraping the sides of the bowl.

3 Before you do any more mixing, tip the cornflakes
onto the plate and crush them up a bit with your hand
– this will make it easier for them to stick to the dough.

4 Add the flour to the creamed butter mixture and mix
in with the wooden spoon to start with, and then with
your hands, to make a soft but not sticky dough.

5 Divide the dough into 16 equal portions. Roll one
portion into a neat ball, then roll it in the cornflakes to
coat completely. Set it on a baking sheet. Repeat with
the rest of the dough to make 16 hairy-looking cookies.
Set them about 2.5cm apart on the baking sheets.

6 Place in the heated oven and bake for 15–17 minutes
until golden. Wearing oven gloves, remove the sheets
from the oven and set them on the wire rack. Leave the
cookies until they are cold before lifting off the sheets.

7 Sandwich them in pairs with your favourite spread
or jam, covering the smooth side of one cookie and
sticking it to the smooth side of another cookie. Store
in an airtight container and eat within 4 days.

Makes 6 huge cookies
GIANT COOKIES

125g unsalted butter, at
  room temperature*
75g light brown muscovado sugar
75g caster sugar
½ teaspoon vanilla extract
1 egg, at room temperature,
  lightly beaten*
150g plain flour
½ teaspoon baking powder
PLUS 150g of your choice of extras:
  choc chips OR chopped nuts
  OR dried fruit OR mini sweeties

YOU WILL ALSO NEED

✳ Large bowl for mixing ✳ wooden
spoon or hand-held electric mixer
✳ plastic or rubber scraper ✳ small
bowl ✳ fork ✳ large metal spoon
✳ 2 baking sheets, lined with baking
paper (if you only have one baking
sheet, you can bake the cookies in
batches, see page 95) ✳ wire rack

ICED COOKIES

The cold cookies can be
decorated with ready-made icing
from squeezy tubes and your
choice of extras: more mini
sweeties or chocolate chips, or
ready-made sugar decorations.
Leave to set on baking paper.

These are the perfect cookies – crisp around
the edges and slightly chewy in the centre,
and really big!

1 Preheat the oven to 180°C/350°F/gas 4. Put the soft
butter, both sugars and the vanilla into a large mixing
bowl and beat with the wooden spoon or electric mixer
for about 2 minutes until the mixture is creamy, smooth
and fluffy* (page 38). Scrape down the sides
of the bowl every now and then so the ingredients
get well mixed.

2 Add the egg to the butter mixture and beat well for 2
minutes, scraping down the sides of the bowl as before.

3 Add the flour and baking powder to the bowl and
mix in with the wooden spoon until everything is
completely blended.

4 Tip all of your chosen extras into the bowl and mix
thoroughly into the cookie dough so they are evenly
distributed. You can use your hands for this.

5 Divide the mixture into 6 equal portions. Using your
hands, shape each into a large, rough, sticky ball (almost
the size of a tennis ball) and drop onto the lined baking
sheets. During baking the mixture will spread to make
cookies about 13cm across, so leave plenty of room
around each one.

6 Place in the heated oven and bake for 15–20 minutes
until golden brown and slightly darker around the
edges. Wearing oven gloves, remove the baking sheets
from the oven and set them on the wire rack. Leave the
cookies to cool completely. Store in an airtight container
and eat within 4 days.

Makes 15
CHOCO SHORTBREAD

100g unsalted butter,
   at room temperature*
50g caster sugar
110g plain flour
40g cocoa powder
2 tablespoons demerara sugar
   OR large sugar crystals
   OR chopped nuts
icing sugar or caster sugar,
   for sprinkling (optional)

YOU WILL ALSO NEED
✱ Large bowl for mixing ✱ wooden spoon or hand-held electric mixer ✱ clingfilm ✱ chopping board ✱ large sharp knife ✱ baking sheet, lined with baking paper ✱ wire rack ✱ sieve or tea strainer

No one will be able to resist these rich, buttery and chocolatey shortbread. The dough is shaped into a log and rolled in sugar (or nuts) for a crunchy exterior. Good for ice-cream sandwiches.

1 Preheat the oven to 160°C/325°F/gas 3. Put the soft butter and caster sugar into the mixing bowl and beat them together with the wooden spoon or electric mixer for a few minutes until creamy and fluffy* (page 38).

2 Add the flour and cocoa powder to the bowl. Use the wooden spoon to mix them into the butter mixture for a minute or so. When it becomes difficult to mix with the spoon, use your hands and press the mixture together to make a ball of dough that is uniformly chocolate brown.

3 Tip the ball of dough out onto a worktop. Shape into a log 15cm long and 5cm wide. Scatter the demerara sugar or chopped nuts in an even layer on a large sheet of clingfilm. Roll the dough log in the sugar or nuts to coat all over. Gently press the sugar or nuts onto the dough with your fingertips so they stick.

4 Set the log on the chopping board and carefully cut across into 15 thick, even slices using the large sharp knife. Lay the slices side by side on the lined baking sheet, about 3cm apart to allow for spreading.

5 Place in the oven and bake for about 20 minutes until the biscuits are slightly darker around the edges. Wearing oven gloves, remove the baking sheet from the oven and set it on the wire rack. Leave the shortbreads until completely cold.

6 Generously sprinkle the shortbreads with sugar (if using icing sugar, sift* it over the shortbreads). Store in an airtight tin and eat within 4 days.

EASY MACARONS

2 large eggs, at room temperature,
  the yolks and whites separated*
good pinch of salt
60g caster sugar
65g ground almonds
80g icing sugar
3 tablespoons cocoa powder

FOR THE FILLING
75g good-quality white chocolate*
75ml whipping cream
10g unsalted butter, at room
  temperature*

YOU WILL ALSO NEED
✳ Large, very clean bowl for mixing
✳ small bowl ✳ hand-held electric
mixer ✳ large sieve ✳ large metal
spoon ✳ baking sheet, lined with
baking paper ✳ 2 medium spoons
✳ wire rack ✳ rolling pin ✳ heatproof
bowl ✳ microwave-proof jug
or saucepan ✳ wooden spoon
✳ table knife

Technique
Whisking and folding
egg whites

The best Mother's Day bake: chocolate
macarons sandwiched with a white chocolate
and cream filling that is called ganache. They
look and taste as if they've come from a fancy
pastry shop but they are easy if you have an
electric mixer. Buy or make a pretty box to
present them!

1 You only need the egg whites, so keep the yolks for
another recipe. Add the salt to the egg whites and whisk*
with the electric mixer on full power until the whites are
opaque and very thick and will stand up in soft peaks
that just flop over a little when the whisk is lifted out*.

2 Whisk in the caster sugar a spoonful at a time. By
the time all the sugar has been whisked in, the whites
should be able to stand up in stiff peaks* when the
whisk is lifted out of the bowl. If not, whisk for a further
20 seconds.

3 Hold the sieve over the bowl and tip the ground
almonds, icing sugar and cocoa powder into it. Sift*
them into the bowl over the egg whites by gently
shaking the sieve or tapping it with your hand.

4 Using the edge of the large metal spoon, gently cut
down through the whites, folding* everything together
– take your time and do this gently so you don't lose any
of the air you've whisked in – until there are no white
streaks in the chocolate meringue mixture.

5 Draw 20 circles that are 5cm across on the baking
paper (use a biscuit cutter or glass to draw around),
then turn the paper over on the baking sheet.

Turn over the page

117

6 Use 2 spoons to dollop the meringue mixture into the circles (one spoon to scoop the mixture and the other to gently scrape it off). Keep the mounds inside the drawn circles.

7 Lift up the baking sheet, then bang it down on the worktop to get rid of any air bubbles in the mixture. Leave to stand for 30 minutes so the macarons can form a 'skin'. Preheat the oven to 180°C/350°F/gas 4.

8 Bake the macarons for 15–20 minutes until they feel firm when gently pressed with a fingertip. Remove the sheet from the oven. Lift the macarons, on the sheet of baking paper, onto the wire rack and leave until cold.

9 Meanwhile, make the filling. Use the rolling pin to bash up the chocolate into small pieces and put it into the heatproof bowl. Heat the cream either in the jug in the microwave or in the saucepan over low heat until bubbles start to appear around the edge. (If microwaving, check the progress every 10 seconds.) Carefully pour the hot cream over the chocolate.

10 Leave for 2 minutes, then add the butter and stir gently until smooth and melted. Allow to cool until the mixture is thick enough to spread.

11 Peel the macarons off the baking paper and sandwich in pairs: use the table knife to spread the filling over the smooth side of one cookie and stick the smooth side of the other cookie onto this. Store in a covered container at room temperature (the macarons taste even better the next day) and eat within 4 days.

Makes 16
ROCKY ROADS

FOR THE BISCUIT BASE
200g plain flour
70g caster sugar
125g unsalted butter,
    cold from the fridge
1 egg
2 tablespoons milk

FOR THE TOPPING
150g milk or dark chocolate
    OR a mix of both
25g unsalted butter
75g mini marshmallows
75g milk or white chocolate sweets
    (e.g. Maltesers)

YOU WILL ALSO NEED
✷ Large bowl for mixing ✷ table knife
✷ small bowl ✷ fork ✷ 20.5cm square
tin, greased with butter ✷ cutting
board ✷ rolling pin ✷ heatproof bowl
✷ medium saucepan ✷ small spoon
✷ disposable piping bag (optional)
✷ small sharp knife

Perfect for a party, these crunchy bites have a shortbread biscuit base plus melted chocolate and lots of marshmallows and sweets. If you want you could also add chocolate-covered raisins or brazil nuts, whole toasted almonds or pecan halves, or even chunks of home-made honeycomb (see page 128).

1 Preheat the oven to 190°C/375°F/gas 5. Put the flour and sugar into the large mixing bowl and mix them together with your hands. Cut the butter into small pieces about the size of your thumbnail and add to the bowl. Toss the mixture with your hands so the pieces of butter get coated in flour. Rub the flour and butter together with your fingertips until the mixture looks like small pieces of rubble (this is rubbing in*, see page 92).

2 Crack the egg against the side of the small bowl and separate* the yolk from the white, putting the yolk into the bowl (the white can be kept in a covered container in the fridge or freezer for another recipe). Wash your hands.

3 Add the milk to the egg yolk and mix with the fork for a couple of seconds. Pour this mixture into the big bowl and stir everything together with the table knife. When the mixture comes together in clumps, put the knife aside and use your hands to finish mixing.

4 Crumble the mixture into the greased tin and press it onto the base in an even layer – you can use your hands or the back of a spoon.

5 Place in the heated oven and bake for 20–25 minutes until lightly golden and the edges are turning brown. Wearing oven gloves, remove the tin from the oven and set on a heatproof surface. Leave to cool.

6 When the biscuit base is cold, run the tip of the table knife around the inside of the tin to loosen the base, then carefully tip it out onto the board. Turn the biscuit base right side up again.

7 Use the rolling pin to break or bash up the chocolate into small pieces. Put them in the heatproof bowl with the butter and melt over a pan of boiling water*. When the chocolate mixture is smooth and melted, carefully lift the bowl off the pan and set it on a heatproof surface.

8 Spread about a third of the chocolate over the base using the table knife. Quickly scatter the marshmallows and chosen extras over the top and gently press them onto the chocolate so they stick.

9 Drizzle the rest of the chocolate in zigzags, squiggles or loops over the top. Leave until the chocolate is set and firm, then cut into 16 squares with the small sharp knife. Store in an airtight tin and eat within 4 days.

CHRISTMAS BAUBLES

350g plain flour
1 tablespoon ground ginger
½ teaspoon ground mixed spice
1 teaspoon bicarbonate of soda
175g unsalted butter
4 tablespoons golden syrup
150g light muscovado sugar

TO DECORATE
100g icing sugar OR ready-made
   piping icing
edible food colouring paste or gel,
   silver or gold edible decorations,
   edible glitter, coloured sugar,
   edible sprinkles, shimmer spray

YOU WILL ALSO NEED
✱ Sieve ✱ large heatproof bowl
for mixing ✱ medium saucepan
✱ wooden spoon ✱ rolling pin ✱ round
biscuit cutter about 6.5cm ✱ fish slice
✱ 1–2 baking sheets, lined with baking
paper (if you only have one baking
sheet, you can bake the biscuits in
batches, see page 95) ✱ wooden
cocktail sticks ✱ wire rack ✱ medium
bowl ✱ plastic or rubber scraper
✱ medium spoon ✱ disposable piping
bag or squeezy icing bottle ✱ kitchen
scissors ✱ thin ribbon (or coloured
string or raffia for threading).

For Christmas why not bake decorations you can eat? Made from the same cookie dough you use for gingerbread people, your baubles can be any shape you fancy and decorated with piped icing, edible gold stars or silver balls – even shimmer spray for a glamorous finish. Hang them from fine ribbons, on the tree or anywhere in the house.

1 Preheat the oven to 180°C/350°F/gas 4. Sift* the flour, ginger, mixed spice and bicarbonate of soda into the mixing bowl.

2 Put the butter, syrup and sugar in the saucepan and warm gently over low heat, stirring frequently with the wooden spoon, until the butter melts. Wearing oven gloves, pour the mixture into the bowl with the flour. Mix well with the wooden spoon to make a firm dough.

3 Sprinkle a little flour on the worktop and tip the dough out onto it. Leave until it just feels pleasantly warm, then gently squeeze and press the mixture with your hands to make a neat ball. Cool for a few more minutes until cold.

4 Sprinkle flour on your rolling pin and the worktop, then roll out* the dough to a large rectangle about 32 x 36cm and just a bit thicker than a pound coin. If the dough cracks, just press it back together; if the mixture starts to crumble, shape it back into a ball between your warm hands and roll out again.

Turn over the page

5 Dip the cutter in flour, then start to cut out discs. Use a fish slice to transfer them to the lined baking sheets, setting the discs slightly apart.

6 Use a cocktail stick to make a small hole in each disc for the ribbon – the hole should be about 1cm in from the edge and 3–4mm across (wiggle the stick around in the hole). Gather up all the dough scraps and squeeze them in your hands so the dough softens, then roll it out as you did before. Cut out more discs.

7 Place in the heated oven and bake for 10–12 minutes until the edges of the discs are turning golden. Wearing oven gloves, carefully remove the sheets from the oven and set them on a heatproof surface.

8 Without touching the discs with your fingers, gently wiggle the cocktail stick in each hole so it is the right size for your ribbon (it may have closed up slightly during baking). Leave the discs to cool and firm up for 10 minutes, then lift them, on the baking paper, onto the wire rack to cool completely.

9 If you're going to make your own glacé icing, sift* the icing sugar into the medium bowl. Add 1 tablespoon cold water and stir to make a smooth, slightly runny icing. If you want to colour it, dip a cocktail stick into the small pot of gel or paste and add just a dot of colouring to begin with (you can add more if the colour isn't right). Stir well until the colour is even with no streaks.

10 To pipe with a disposable icing bag, fill the bag with the icing*, then snip off the tip with kitchen scissors so the opening is 3–4mm across (page 32). Alternatively, spoon the icing into a squeezy icing bottle and screw on the tip.

11 Hold the bag or bottle upright in one hand over the top of a disc (making sure the top end of the bag is still firmly twisted) and squeeze gently to pipe shapes – dots, initials, stars or whatever you fancy. Before the icing starts to set, stick on edible decorations. Leave for 1–2 hours until completely set and dry before threading ribbon through the holes.

Makes 16
JAM CRUMBLES

125g plain flour
125g wholemeal plain flour
100g caster sugar
1 ½ teaspoons baking powder
150g unsalted butter,
    cold from the fridge
2 eggs – the yolk and white of
    1 egg separated* into 2 bowls
about 3 tablespoons raspberry
    or strawberry jam

YOU WILL ALSO NEED
✱ Large bowl for mixing ✱ table
knife ✱ small bowl ✱ fork ✱ wooden
spoon ✱ 2 baking trays, lined with
baking paper (if you only have one
baking sheet, you can bake the
cookies in batches, see page 95)
✱ small spoon

Rich and crumbly with a jam-filled thumbprint centre, these are fun to make.

1 Preheat the oven to 200°C/400°F/gas 6. Put the two flours, the sugar and baking powder into the large mixing bowl and mix well with your hands.

2 Cut the butter into small pieces about the size of your thumbnail and add to the bowl. Gently mix them in so they get covered in the flour mixture. Rub the flour and butter together with your fingertips until the mixture looks like small pieces of rubble (this is rubbing in*, page 92).

3 You need a whole egg plus a yolk, so save the extra egg white in the fridge or freezer for another recipe. Beat* the egg and yolk together with the fork for a few seconds, then tip into the mixing bowl. Mix using the wooden spoon until everything starts to come together, then use your hands to press the mixture into a large ball.

4 Turn the ball out onto a worktop and divide into 16 evenly sized pieces. Roll each piece into a ball and set on the lined baking sheets. Make sure that the balls are at least 5cm apart as they will spread during baking.

5 Dip your thumb in flour, then press it into the middle of each ball to make a good hollow. Spoon a little jam – about ½ teaspoon – into each hollow.

6 Place in the heated oven and bake for about 15 minutes until golden. Wearing oven gloves, remove the baking sheets from the oven and set them on a heatproof surface. Leave the crumbles to cool before lifting them off – don't eat while hot as the jam will burn your tongue. Store in an airtight container and eat within 4 days.

Makes 16
HONEYCOMB CRUNCHIES

FOR THE HONEYCOMB
1 teaspoon bicarbonate of soda
75g caster sugar
2 tablespoons golden syrup
   (measured flat not rounded)*

TO ASSEMBLE
250g dark or milk chocolate,
   or a mixture
100g unsalted butter, cut
   into 1cm cubes
2 tablespoons golden syrup
150g digestive biscuits

YOU WILL ALSO NEED
✳ Wire whisk ✳ baking tray, oiled
✳ deep, medium-sized heavy-based
saucepan ✳ wooden spoon ✳ rolling
pin ✳ large heatproof bowl ✳ table
knife ✳ 20.5cm square tin, lined
with baking paper ✳ clingfilm
✳ small sharp knife

Honeycomb is the most amazing stuff – add the bicarbonate of soda to the sugar and watch as it explodes in the pan and grows before your eyes. Add this light, crunchy treat to ice cream sundaes and rocky road or eat it plain.

1 Make the honeycomb first. Have the bicarbonate of soda measured and ready for when you need it, plus the wire whisk and oiled baking tray. Put the sugar and golden syrup into the saucepan and set it on very low heat. Warm gently for 10 minutes until all the sugar has melted, stirring occasionally with the wooden spoon.

2 When the sugar is completely melted, turn up the heat to medium. Once the mixture has started to boil, leave to bubble without stirring until it turns golden brown.

3 Turn off the heat under the pan. Cover one of your hands with a dry tea towel or oven glove for protection, then take hold of the pan handle. Add the bicarbonate of soda and quickly whisk it in for a couple of seconds only. The mixture will froth up massively and you need to take great care as it's extremely hot.

4 Quickly pour it into the middle of the oiled baking tray. Don't spread it out or touch it or the tray. Leave it to cool and harden, which will take about 30 minutes. Wash and dry the saucepan.

Turn over the page

5 Use the rolling pin to break or bash up the chocolate into small pieces. Put them into the heatproof bowl and add the butter and golden syrup. Melt gently*, giving it a stir now and then. When the chocolate mixture is smooth, carefully lift the bowl off the pan and set it on a heatproof surface.

6 Put the biscuits into a plastic bag and use the rolling pin to break them up into chunks the size of your thumbnail. Bash up the set honeycomb into chunks roughly the same size. Add the biscuits and honeycomb to the melted chocolate and mix well so all the chunks are coated.

7 Scoop the whole lot into the lined, square tin and spread it evenly, right into the corners. Cover with clingfilm, then chill in the fridge for about 2 hours until firm and set. Cut into 16 squares with the small sharp knife. Store, tightly covered, in the fridge and eat within 2 days.

It's not difficult – it's chemistry. There are 4 stages to bread making, which we explain in this chapter. It also takes longer, so do leave enough time.

 You need to use 'strong flour' or 'bread flour' for the recipes in this chapter, not the plain or self-raising flour that you use for cakes and biscuits. Strong, or bread flour, has more protein and less starch, so the dough can double in size.

 When you mix a sachet of fast-action dried yeast with flour (never mix it with water) and add warm water, the yeast will spring into action and begin to grow and breathe. They produce millions of tiny bubbles of carbon dioxide which makes the dough swell.

 If your dough doesn't rise, it is because either the yeast is stale (from an opened sachet), past its 'use by' date or because the water was too hot and killed the yeast. Start again!

 Cover the top of the bowl of dough and leave it somewhere cosy, away from draughts – yeast prefers a warm, moist environment for growing.

 Use soft butter to grease the inside of your loaf tin – it will form a barrier so the dough doesn't stick.

EASY BREAD ROLLS

500g strong white bread flour,
   plus extra for sprinkling
1 teaspoon salt
1 x 7g sachet fast-action dried yeast

YOU WILL ALSO NEED
✳ Small saucepan ✳ large bowl
for mixing ✳ clingfilm ✳ table knife
✳ baking sheet, lined with baking
paper ✳ fish slice ✳ wire rack

Technique
Kneading and proving

You can make all sorts of bread from this dough – you can shape it into rolls or a couple of loaves, or add seeds or dried fruit. If you mix it with milk instead of water you'll get softer bread, or you can use another type of bread flour*(though you may need a bit more or a bit less water).

1 Gently warm 300ml water until it is lukewarm*. Put the flour, salt and yeast into the mixing bowl and mix with your hands, then pour in the lukewarm water.

2 Press and squeeze everything together to make a soft but not sticky dough. If the dough feels sticky, and sticks to the sides of the bowl, sprinkle over more flour a tablespoon at a time and mix it in; if there are dry crumbs in the bottom of the bowl and the dough won't stick together, sprinkle over more water a tablespoon at a time and mix in.

3 Sprinkle the worktop and your hands with a little flour, then scoop out the dough. Now start to knead* it: to do this you'll need to use both hands – one to hold down one edge of the dough, and the other hand to stretch out the other end and then gather it all back into a ball again.

4 Turn the ball around and stretch the dough out again, then gather back into a ball and turn it around. Carry on kneading like this for 4 minutes – set the timer.

Turn over the page

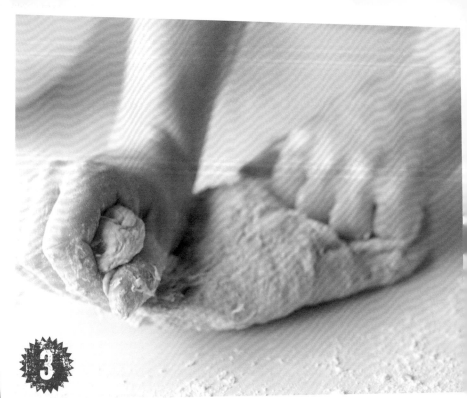

5 Cover the dough with the upside-down bowl (so it doesn't get dry and hard) and leave it for 10 minutes. Uncover the dough and give it another 4 minutes of kneading. You'll see how much easier it is this time, and how smooth and stretchy the dough feels. Put the ball of dough back into the bowl and cover the top with clingfilm so the dough keeps warm and moist while the yeast get to work.

6 Leave for about an hour – the yeast will produce lots of tiny bubbles of air that will make the dough expand to double its original size (this is proving*).

7 Sprinkle the worktop and your hands with flour again, and scoop out the ball of dough. As you touch it, it will start to collapse – this is fine as you want to have millions of very small gas bubbles instead of a few bigger ones (this is knocking back*).

8 Divide the dough into 12 equal portions. You can do this by rolling it into a sausage, then cutting across into 12 equal slices with the table knife. Or you can weigh the ball of dough, then divide it by 12 (this is easy if you have digital scales).

9 Roll each piece into a neat ball in your hands (you could also make sausage shapes). Put them on the lined baking sheet, spacing them about 3cm apart.

10 Cover the sheet loosely with clingfilm, then leave for about 45 minutes – they will expand again to double the size. Towards the end of this time, preheat the oven to 220°C/425°F/gas 7.

11 Uncover the rolls and place in the heated oven. Bake for 15–20 minutes until golden brown. Wearing oven gloves, remove the sheet from the oven and set it on a heatproof surface. Use the fish slice to transfer the rolls to the wire rack and leave to cool. Store in a covered container in a cool spot. Best eaten the same day, or split in half and toasted the next day.

CHEESE ROLLS

Add 100g grated, mature Cheddar to the flour, salt and yeast before you mix in the water (in step 2). You can sprinkle the rolls with a bit more cheese before you bake them too.

Learn to Bake
BREAD 139

BREAD STICKS

FOR THE DOUGH

300g strong white bread flour
  OR 150g each strong white bread
  flour and wholemeal bread flour,
  plus extra for sprinkling
2 teaspoons caster sugar
1 x 7g sachet fast-action dried yeast
¾ teaspoon salt
225ml lukewarm water*

TO FINISH

75g milk or dark chocolate chips
  OR broken bits from a bar
  OR 3 tablespoons sesame seeds
  OR 75g chopped pitted olives

YOU WILL ALSO NEED

✱ Microwave-safe jug or small
saucepan ✱ large bowl for mixing
✱ ruler ✱ small sharp knife ✱ 2 baking
sheets, lined with baking paper (if
you only have one baking sheet, you
can bake the bread sticks in batches,
see page 95) ✱ cling film ✱ fish slice
✱ wire rack

Great for snacks, bread sticks can be soft or crisp, savoury or sweet. Here are some for you to try.

1 Put the flour, sugar, yeast and salt into the mixing bowl. Mix with your hand, then pour in the lukewarm water. Gently press and squeeze everything together until thoroughly combined to make a smooth, soft dough. If there are any dry crumbs in the bottom of the bowl, mix in a little more warm water a tablespoon at a time; if the dough feels sticky and clings to the sides of the bowl, mix in more flour a tablespoon at a time.

2 Lightly sprinkle the worktop with flour, then turn out the dough onto it. Sprinkle your hands with flour. Pat and press the dough out to a rectangle 22 x 30cm.

3 Sprinkle the chocolate OR sesame seeds OR chopped olives evenly over the dough. Starting at one short end, roll up the dough into a spiral, then gently stretch out the roll so it is 34cm long. With your hands, flatten and pat out the roll to make a 16 x 34cm rectangle. Carefully slice the rectangle into 16 strips that are 16cm long.

4 Pick up the first strip and hold one end in each hand. Gently twist the strip, giving it a little stretch, then set it on a lined baking sheet (don't worry if it starts to untwist a bit). Do the same thing with all the strips, setting them about 3cm apart. Cover the sheets loosely with clingfilm and leave for 20 minutes – the strips will puff up. Meanwhile, preheat the oven to 220°C/425°F/gas 7.

5 Uncover the baking sheets and place in the oven. Bake the bread sticks for 12 minutes until golden. If you want them to be crunchy, bake them for an extra 5 minutes.

6 Wearing oven gloves, remove the sheets from the oven and set on a heatproof surface. Transfer the bread sticks to the wire rack and cool. Best eaten the same day.

DEEP-DISH PIZZA

FOR THE DOUGH

500g strong white bread flour
1 teaspoon salt
1 x 7g sachet fast-action dried yeast
2 tablespoons rapeseed or olive oil,
   plus extra for kneading
325ml lukewarm water*

FOR THE TOPPING

8 spicy or Italian-style sausages
2 x 400g tins chopped tomatoes
4 garlic cloves
300g mozzarella
50g pecorino or Parmesan

YOU WILL ALSO NEED

✳ Microwave-safe jug or small
saucepan ✳ large bowl for mixing
✳ clingfilm ✳ baking dish, oiled ✳
large sieve or colander ✳ medium
bowl ✳ chopping board ✳ garlic
crusher ✳ medium spoon
✳ 2 plates ✳ vegetable peeler
✳ small sharp knife ✳ roasting tin
or deep baking tin (about 22 x
30cm), oiled ✳ large sharp knife
or pizza cutter

This isn't your usual pizza with a thin crust
and tiny topping – this is a real pizza pie!

1 Put the flour in the mixing bowl. Add the salt and yeast
and mix together with your hand, then push the flour to
sides of the bowl to make a well in the middle.

2 Pour the oil and lukewarm water into the well. Mix
the flour into the liquids with your hands, then squeeze
everything together to make a dough that feels quite
soft. If the dough feels dry and there are dry crumbs
at the bottom of the bowl, sprinkle over more water
a tablespoon at a time and mix it in.

3 Rub the dough with a little oil, then scoop out the
dough onto the worktop. Knead the dough, by pushing
and stretching it, then folding it over, for 4 minutes
(page 136). Gather into a ball, cover with the upside-
down bowl and take a break for 10 minutes.

4 Uncover the dough and knead again for 4 minutes
until it feels very soft, elastic and smooth. Put the dough
back into the bowl and cover it with clingfilm. Leave for
about 1 hour to prove*– the dough will expand and
double in size.

5 During this time, prepare the topping. Preheat the
oven to 200°C/400°F/gas 6. Put the sausages into the
oiled baking dish and cook in the oven for 20 minutes.
Wearing oven gloves, remove the dish from the oven
and set it on a heatproof surface to cool. Leave the
oven on, but turn it up to 220°C/425°F/gas 7.

6 Set the sieve or colander over the medium-sized bowl,
then pour the chopped tomatoes into the sieve. Leave
them to drain – you want as much of the liquid to drain
off as possible. (Use the liquid for a soup or pasta sauce.)

Turn over the page

7 Place the garlic on the chopping board and bash with the underside of the small saucepan, then remove the papery covering on the garlic. Put the peeled garlic into the garlic crusher and crush it through the holes into the bowl of tomatoes. Stir to mix.

8 Drain the mozzarella (it comes packed in liquid), then pull apart into long strands and put onto a plate. Use the vegetable peeler to 'peel' or shave strips from the pecorino or Parmesan onto the other plate. Put the cooked sausages on the chopping board and carefully cut across into slices about 1.5cm thick.

9 When the dough is ready, scoop it out of the bowl straight into the oiled roasting tin. With your hands, press out so it covers the base of the tin, then press it up the sides using your thumbs – the dough will be very elastic and will keep springing back, but do your best. Leave it for 10 minutes to relax a little, then press it firmly into the corners and right up the sides of the tin. Make sure the dough is the same thickness everywhere.

10 Place the tin in the oven and bake the pizza base for 10 minutes so it starts to set (this helps prevent it from going soggy when you add the topping). Wearing oven gloves, remove the tin and set it on a heatproof surface.

11 Scatter the mozzarella strands over the pizza base (don't forget the tin will be hot). Next add the sausage slices, make sure they are evenly distributed so everyone gets their fair share. Spoon over the tomatoes. Finally, arrange the cheese shavings over the top.

12 Carefully return the tin to the oven and bake for 25 minutes until the crust is golden brown and the filling is bubbling. Wearing oven gloves, lift out the tin and set it on a heatproof surface. Leave the pizza to settle for 10 minutes (this makes it easier to cut), then cut into 8 squares.

MAKE IT VEGGY

Replace the sausages with 2 x 400g tins artichoke hearts in water. Drain the artichokes really well, then cut each one in 4. Put onto the pizza in place of the sausage slices.

Makes 12
HOT X BUNS

350g strong white bread flour,
   plus extra for sprinkling
100g wholemeal bread flour
¾ teaspoon salt
3 tablespoons caster sugar
2 teaspoons ground mixed spice
1 x 7g sachet fast-action dried yeast
50g unsalted butter, at room
   temperature*
125g dried mixed fruit
2 eggs, at room temperature*
175ml lukewarm milk*

TO FINISH
4 tablespoons strong
   white bread flour
2 tablespoons runny honey

YOU WILL ALSO NEED
✱ Large bowl for mixing ✱ small
saucepan ✱ fork ✱ clingfilm ✱ table
knife ✱ baking sheet, lined with
baking paper ✱ small bowl ✱ small
spoon ✱ disposable piping bag or
small plastic bag ✱ pastry brush
✱ wire rack

These smell so good in the oven it's hard to wait until they'll cool enough to eat! Each little bun is decorated with a flour and water cross piped on just before baking, and a sticky glaze is added afterwards. You could also make a huge bun with the same mixture.

1 Put both kinds of flour into the mixing bowl, then drop the salt, sugar, mixed spice and yeast on top. Mix everything together really well with your hands.

2 Drop the butter into the bowl. Using your fingertips, rub in* butter and flour (page 92). Add the dried fruit and mix in with your hands.

3 Add the eggs to the milk and beat* with the fork for a few seconds to break up the yolks and mix everything together. Pour into the flour mixture and gently press and squeeze everything together with your hands until it is thoroughly combined. If there are dry crumbs at the bottom of the bowl and the dough won't stick together, sprinkle over more milk, a tablespoon at a time, and mix it in; if the dough is very sticky and sticks to the sides of the bowl, mix in more flour, a tablespoon at a time.

4 Sprinkle the worktop and your hands with a little flour, then tip out the dough onto the worktop. Using both hands, knead* the dough thoroughly, by pushing and stretching it, then folding it over, for 4 minutes (page 136).

5 Cover the dough with the upside-down bowl and leave it to have a rest for 10 minutes. Then uncover the dough and give it another 4 minutes of kneading until it feels very soft, elastic and smooth.

CHERRIES & BERRIES

If you're not so keen on raisins, currants and sultanas, use a pack of dried berries and cherries instead.

GIANT HOT X BUNS

Instead of dividing the dough into 12 pieces, shape it with your hands into one large ball about 15cm across. Rub the inside of a 20.5cm sandwich tin with soft butter, then set the ball in the centre. Cover loosely with a sheet of clingfilm and leave to rise until the dough has puffed up and expanded so it almost fills the tin. Pipe the paste over the ball to make a cross, then bake for 30 minutes until golden brown. Wearing oven gloves, remove from the oven and turn out onto a wire rack. Turn the bun the right way up, so the cross is on top, then brush with the honey glaze.

6 Put the dough back into the bowl and cover it with clingfilm. Leave it on the worktop for about an hour to prove* – it will expand so it is doubled in size (page 136).

7 Sprinkle the worktop with a very little flour again, then tip out the dough and divide it into 12 equal pieces – you can do this using digital scales, weighing the whole ball of dough first, or flatten it into a disc and then cut it into 12 segments with the table knife.

8 Shape each piece of dough into a neat ball by rolling it in your hands. Put the balls on the lined baking sheet, making sure they are about 3cm apart. Cover them very lightly with a sheet of clingfilm, then leave for about 40 minutes – they'll expand and double in size.

9 After 20 minutes, preheat the oven to 200°C/400°F/ gas 6. Then make the paste for the cross: put the flour in the small bowl, add 3 tablespoons cold water and stir to make a smooth, thick mixture that's just runny enough to be piped like icing. Spoon it into a disposable piping bag or small plastic bag and snip off the tip. Uncover the buns and pipe a cross on top of each one.

10 Place in the heated oven and bake for 15 minutes until golden brown. Wearing oven gloves, lift out the baking sheet and set it on a heatproof surface.

11 Put the honey into the washed and dried small bowl and stir in 1 tablespoon hot water from the kettle to make a runny syrup. Brush over the hot buns to give them a sticky glaze. Transfer the buns to the wire rack and leave to cool. Store in a covered container in a cool spot and eat the same day, or split and toast the next day.

Makes 12
PITA POCKETS

450g strong white bread flour
1 teaspoon salt
1 x 7g sachet fast-action dried yeast
1 tablespoon rapeseed or olive oil,
   plus extra for kneading
275ml lukewarm water*

YOU WILL ALSO NEED
✱ Microwave-safe jug or small
saucepan ✱ large bowl for mixing
✱ clingfilm ✱ table knife ✱ rolling pin
✱ 2 baking sheets, non-stick or lightly
greased with butter (if you only have
one baking sheet, you can bake the
breads in batches*, see page 95)
✱ small bowl ✱ fish slice (optional)
✱ wire rack, covered with a dry
tea towel

You can watch these round, soft pitas puff up in
the oven as they bake at mega heat. When split
open, they make a pocket you can fill. Or use
them to scoop up dips.

1 Put the flour, salt and dried yeast into the mixing bowl.
Mix well together with your hands, then make a well in
the centre by pushing the flour to the sides of the bowl.

2 Pour the oil and lukewarm water into the well. Stick
the fingers of one hand into the oily water in the well
and use them to froth up the liquid. Gradually whisk
the flour into the liquids with your fingers. When the
mixture starts to get too thick to do this any more, use
your whole hand to gently press and squeeze everything
together to make a soft but not sticky dough.

3 If the dough feels sticky, and sticks to the sides of
the bowl, mix in more flour a tablespoon at a time; if
the dough is hard and dry, and there are dry crumbs
at the bottom of the bowl, sprinkle over more water,
a tablespoon at a time, and mix in.

4 Pour about a tablespoon of oil onto the worktop
and rub it over the surface with your hands. Tip out
the dough onto the oiled surface and cover it with the
upside-down bowl. Leave it to rest for 5 minutes.

5 Uncover the dough. With both hands, knead* it
thoroughly, by pushing and stretching it, then folding
it over, for 4 minutes (page 136). Cover with the bowl
and leave for 10 minutes.

Turn over the page

6 Uncover the dough and knead for another 4 minutes until it feels very soft, elastic and smooth. Put the dough back into the bowl and cover it with clingfilm. Leave for about 1 hour to prove*– the dough will expand and double in size.

7 Tip out the dough onto the worktop (you might need to add a tiny bit of oil, but only enough to prevent the dough from sticking). Punch it down with your knuckles so it deflates*. Divide the dough into 12 equal pieces – you can do this using digital scales, weighing the whole ball of dough first, or flatten it into a disc and then cut it into 12 segments with the table knife.

8 Shape each piece into a neat ball with your hands. Cover loosely with a sheet of clingfilm and leave to rest on the worktop for 10 minutes.

9 With the rolling pin, roll out each ball into a flat disc about 15cm across. Set the discs about 2cm apart on the baking sheets. Cover lightly with clingfilm and leave for 25 minutes – the discs will puff up a bit. Meanwhile, preheat the oven to its maximum setting.

10 Uncover the pita breads. Dip your fingers in a bowl of cold water and flick water over the breads. Then open the oven door carefully (there'll be a rush of very hot air), place the baking sheets in the oven and bake the pitas for 3–4 minutes until puffed and lightly browned around the edges.

11 Wearing oven gloves, remove the sheets from the oven and set on a heatproof surface. Transfer the breads to the wire rack by sliding them off the sheet or using a fish slice, and cover with another dry tea towel. Eat warm or lightly toasted the same or the next day.

EXTRA FLAVOUR

After you have kneaded the dough for the first time and given it a rest in step 5, sprinkle 2 tablespoons chopped fresh herbs (coriander/parsley) OR chopped pitted olives over the dough and knead in. Continue as in the main recipe.

Makes 12
ICED FINGERS

450g strong white bread flour, plus
    extra for sprinkling
¾ teaspoon salt
4 tablespoons caster sugar
1 x 7g sachet fast-action dried yeast
50g unsalted butter, at room
    temperature*
1 egg, at room temperature*
225ml lukewarm milk*

TO FINISH
4 tablespoons seedless raspberry jam
200g icing sugar (or 400g, if you
    want to personalise the iced fingers
    with piped names)
edible food colouring (optional)

YOU WILL ALSO NEED
✸ Microwave-safe jug or small
saucepan ✸ large bowl for mixing
✸ fork ✸ clingfilm ✸ table knife
✸ baking sheet, lined with baking
paper ✸ fish slice ✸ wire rack ✸ small
spoon ✸ squeezy icing bottles or
disposable piping bags ✸ small bowl

Milk and butter added to a sweet white
dough make these fingers very soft, perfect
for injecting with jam and decorating with
glacé icing – white or any colour you like.

1 Put the flour, salt, sugar and yeast into the mixing
bowl and stir them together well with your hand. Add
the butter to the flour mixture and rub together between
your fingertips and thumbs until you can't see any
lumps or bumps in the mixture.

2 Add the egg to the lukewarm milk and beat* with
the fork for a couple of seconds just to break up the
yolk and mix everything together.

3 Pour the milk mix into the bowl with the flour and
gently press and squeeze everything together until it
is thoroughly combined to make a soft but not sticky
dough. If the dough feels sticky, and sticks to the sides
of the bowl, sprinkle over more flour a tablespoon at a
time and mix it in; if the dough is dry and hard, or there
are dry crumbs at the bottom of the bowl, sprinkle over
more milk a tablespoon at a time and mix in.

4 Sprinkle a little flour over the worktop and your
fingers, then tip out the dough onto the worktop. With
both hands, knead* the dough thoroughly, by pushing
and stretching it, then folding it over, for 4 minutes
(page 136). Cover with the upside-down bowl and
leave to rest for 10 minutes.

5 Uncover the dough and give it another 4 minutes
of kneading until it feels very soft, elastic and smooth.
Then put the dough back into the bowl and cover it with
clingfilm. Leave for about 1 hour to prove*– the dough
will expand so it is doubled in size.

Turn over the page

6 Turn out the dough onto the floured worktop again and divide it into 12 equal pieces – you can do this using digital scales, weighing the whole ball of dough first, or flatten it into a disc and then cut it into 12 segments with the table knife.

7 Shape each piece into a ball, then with your hands roll it on the worktop into a sausage about 12cm long. Set the sausages about 2cm apart on the lined baking sheet. Cover the sheet loosely with clingfilm and leave for about 45 minutes – the sausages will expand and double in size. Towards the end of this rising time, preheat the oven to 220°C/425°F/gas 7.

8 Uncover the fingers and place in the heated oven. Bake for 10–12 minutes until golden brown. Wearing oven gloves, remove the sheet from the oven and set it on a heatproof surface. Use the fish slice to transfer the fingers to the wire rack and leave them to cool.

9 Give the jam a good stir, then spoon it into a squeezy bottle. Push the nozzle of the bottle into the middle of one long side of a finger and squeeze in or inject a little jam (about a teaspoon). Repeat with the other fingers.

10 Put 200g icing sugar and 2 tablespoons water in the small bowl and stir to make a smooth icing that just runs off the back of the spoon when you lift it out of the bowl.

11 Spoon the icing over the cooled fingers, using the back of the spoon to push the icing along the top of each finger. Leave to set.

12 You can personalise your iced fingers, if you like: make up another batch of icing following the method in step 10. Stir in a few drops of edible food colouring. Spoon the icing into a squeezy bottle or disposable piping bag. Pipe names or zigzags of icing over the top of each finger. Leave to set before serving. Best the same or the next day.

JAMMY SPLITS

If you don't fancy injecting the jam or icing the fingers, carefully split the fingers in half using a table knife and spread the cut surfaces with jam or your favourite spread, then finish with a generous sprinkle of icing sugar.

PLAITED TREACLE LOAF

750g strong white bread flour,
   plus extra for sprinkling
5g salt
1 x 7g sachet fast-action dried yeast
1 tablespoon black treacle
1 tablespoon rapeseed or olive oil
450ml lukewarm water*
1 ½ tablespoons sesame seeds
   (optional)

YOU WILL ALSO NEED

✴ Microwave-safe jug or small
saucepan ✴ large bowl for mixing
✴ small bowl ✴ small spoon ✴ table
knife ✴ 900g loaf tin (about 26 x
12.5 x 7.5cm), greased with butter
✴ wire rack

A small amount of black treacle turns this dough an off-white colour (not black) and gives it a very slightly sweet, nutty taste. There's an easy way to plait it too, so the top looks special. The loaf is great for sandwiches and toast (ask people to guess the secret ingredient!).

1 Put the flour into the mixing bowl. Add the salt and the dried yeast and mix everything together very well with your hands.

2 Measure the treacle and oil into the small bowl. Pour in half of the lukewarm water and stir just until the treacle has dissolved. Pour the treacle mixture and the rest of the lukewarm water into the bowl with the flour.

3 Put your hands into the bowl and mix the liquids into the dry ingredients, gently pressing and squeezing everything together, to make a soft but not sticky dough. If the dough feels really sticky and sticks to the bowl, sprinkle a tablespoon of flour on top and mix it in; if there are dry bits at the bottom of the bowl and the dough feels stiff and dry, sprinkle an extra tablespoon of lukewarm water over the dough and mix it in.

4 Sprinkle a little flour on the worktop and tip out the dough onto it. Using both hands, knead* the dough, by pushing and stretching it, then folding it over, for 4 minutes (page 136). Cover the dough with the upside-down bowl and leave it to rest for 10 minutes.

Turn over the page

5 Uncover the dough and give it another 4 minutes of kneading until it feels very soft, elastic and smooth. Cover it with the bowl again and leave to rest for another 10 minutes.

6 Uncover the dough and pat it out to a thick rectangle that is about 1cm bigger all around than your loaf tin. With the table knife, cut the rectangle down its length into 3 wide strips, leaving them joined at one end.

7 Now plait the 3 strips together: lift the strip on the left up over the one in the middle (so it becomes the middle strip), then lift the strip on the right up over the middle one (so this then becomes the middle strip). Repeat, starting with the strip on the left each time. When you get to the end, pinch the ends together and tuck them under the plait.

8 Sprinkle half of the sesame seeds over the base and sides of the buttered tin. Carefully lift the plait into the tin (if the ends escape, tuck them underneath so the loaf looks neat). Sprinkle with the rest of the seeds.

9 Slip the tin into a large, clean plastic bag and flap the ends so the bag inflates like a balloon, then tie the ends – the air inside will stop the plastic sticking to the dough as it expands. Leave for about an hour to prove*– the dough will rise and double in size. Towards the end of this time, preheat the oven to 220°C/425°F/gas 7.

10 Take the tin out of the plastic bag and carefully put it into the heated oven. Bake for 35 minutes until golden brown. Wearing oven gloves, lift the tin out of the oven and tip the loaf onto the wire rack so it is upside down. Use the knocking test* to see if the bread is cooked all the way through; if necessary, put the loaf back into the oven – straight onto the oven shelf, not back in its tin – and bake for 5 more minutes, then test again.

11 Once you're sure it's thoroughly cooked, turn the loaf the right way up on the wire rack and leave it cool. Best eaten within 5 days.

Makes 1 large loaf
SLEEPOVER LOAF

500g strong white bread flour,
   plus extra for sprinkling
1 teaspoon salt
1 tablespoon caster sugar
¼ teaspoon fast-action dried yeast
   (from a 7g sachet)
100g dried sour cherries OR dried
   cranberries OR jumbo raisins
150g pecan halves OR roughly
   chopped hazelnuts, almonds,
   macadamia or brazil nuts
100g bar dark or milk chocolate,
   broken up, OR choc chips
420ml water from the cold tap

YOU WILL ALSO NEED
✴ Large bowl for mixing ✴ rolling
pin ✴ wooden spoon (optional)
✴ clingfilm ✴ plastic or rubber scraper
✴ 900g loaf tin (about 26 x 12.5 x
7.5cm), greased with butter
✴ wire rack

This easy loaf needs no kneading – you just mix it up and leave it to 'sleepover' in your kitchen when you go to bed. Then next morning you can bake it and eat thick slices spread with cream cheese.

1 Put the flour, salt, sugar, yeast and dried fruit into the mixing bowl. Snap the pecan halves in half with your fingers and add to the bowl with the chocolate. Give everything a really good mix with your hands.

2 Pour in the cold water and mix well with your hands or the wooden spoon until thoroughly combined – the mixture will be incredibly sticky and a bit heavy.

3 Cover the bowl with clingfilm and leave it on the worktop overnight or for about 12 hours. While you're sleeping the dough will be getting active – next morning it will look puffed up and covered with little bubbles.

4 Sprinkle the worktop and your hands with a little flour, then scoop out the dough. It will feel soft and sticky. Gently fold it half and then in half again. Scoop it up once more and drop it into the buttered tin. Gently press into the corners so it has an even shape. The tin should be about half full. Cover loosely with clingfilm and leave for about 1 ½ hours to prove*– the dough will rise up so it almost reaches the top of the tin. Towards the end of the rising time, preheat the oven to 220°C/425°F/gas 7.

5 Uncover the loaf and carefully place it in the heated oven. Bake for 35 minutes until golden brown. Wearing oven gloves, remove the tin from the oven and set it on a heatproof surface. Leave to cool for 10 minutes, then, with the oven gloves on, carefully turn the loaf out of the tin and set it upright on the wire rack. Cool completely before slicing. Best eaten within 4 days.

Makes 8
LARGE SOFT PRETZELS

FOR THE DOUGH

300g strong white bread flour,
    plus extra for sprinkling
2 teaspoons caster sugar
1 x 7g sachet fast-action dried yeast
¾ teaspoon salt
225ml lukewarm milk*
1 large egg

TO FINISH

2–3 tablespoons coarse sugar crystals
    or demerara sugar OR
    3 tablespoons grated cheese
    (e.g. Cheddar or Parmesan)
    OR coarse sea salt or rock salt
30g unsalted butter

YOU WILL ALSO NEED

✱ Microwave-proof jug or small
saucepan ✱ large bowl for mixing
✱ clingfilm ✱ ruler ✱ 2 baking sheets,
lined with baking paper (if you only
have one baking sheet, you can bake
the pretzels in batches*, see page 95)
✱ small bowl ✱ fork ✱ pastry brush
✱ microwave-proof dish (optional)

These soft and chewy pretzels are delicious
with dips and spreads or just on their own.
Once the basic dough is shaped, you can add
your choice of topping.

1 Put the flour, sugar, yeast and salt into the mixing
bowl. Mix well with your hands, then pour in the
lukewarm milk. Use your hands to gently press and
squeeze everything together until thoroughly combined
to make a very smooth, soft dough.

2 If there are any dry crumbs in the bottom of the bowl
and the dough feels hard and dry, mix in a little more
warm milk (or water) a tablespoon at a time; if the dough
feels very sticky and clings to the sides of the bowl mix
in more flour a tablespoon at a time.

3 Lightly sprinkle the worktop with flour, then turn
out the dough onto it. Knead* the dough thoroughly,
by repeatedly pushing and stretching it, then folding
it over, for 5 minutes until it feels very soft, elastic
and smooth.

4 Put the dough back into the bowl and cover it with
clingfilm. Leave at room temperature for 30 minutes
so the dough can rest and rise.

5 Turn out the dough onto the worktop again (don't
sprinkle with flour this time). Divide into 8 equal pieces.
Shape each into a ball – they don't have to be neat –
then leave on the worktop, uncovered, for 5 minutes.

Turn over the page

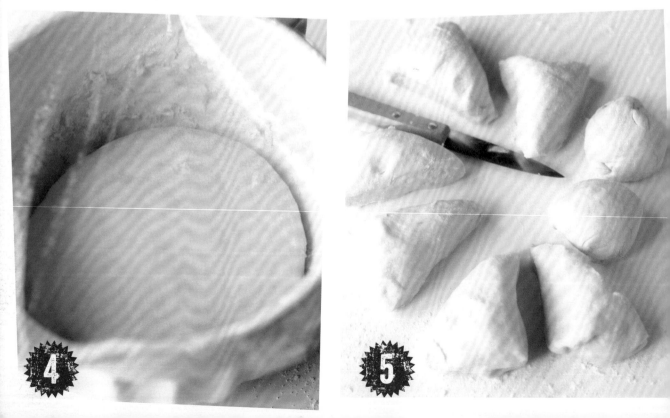

7A

7B

7C

8

9

6 With your hands, roll each ball of dough on the worktop to make a thin sausage about 46cm long. If the dough starts to stick, add a little flour to your hands.

7 To shape each sausage into a pretzel, first bend it into a U. Lift one end and set it on top of the base of the U on the opposite side. Repeat with the other end – the bent 'legs' of the U will now cross in the middle of the shape.

8 Carefully lift the pretzels onto the lined baking sheets, making sure to set them well apart to allow for expansion. Leave uncovered at room temperature for 15 minutes. Meanwhile, preheat the oven to 220°C/425°F/gas 7. Add 1 tablespoon cold water to the egg and beat with the fork for a couple of seconds. Carefully brush this mixture over each pretzel in a thin even layer.

9 Sprinkle the pretzels with your chosen topping, or leave them plain, then place in the heated oven and bake for about 15 minutes until golden brown.

10 While the pretzels are baking, gently melt the butter in the microwave-proof dish in the microwave for about 10 seconds, or in the washed saucepan on top of the stove. Wash the pastry brush and dry on a teatowel. Wearing oven gloves, remove the baking sheets from the oven and set on a heatproof surface. Brush each pretzel with melted butter, which will give them a soft, glossy crust. Leave to cool on the sheets until just warm before eating. Best eaten the same day.

Learn to Bake

PASTRY

Pastry is the opposite of bread – it prefers a cool and chilly environment. For best results, make it when the kitchen is at its coolest and don't skip the chilling steps where the pastry is left to firm up in the fridge.

 If you are using ready-made pastry, read the pack instructions and follow exactly what they say about defrosting or removing the pastry from the fridge.

 When making shortcrust pastry, the 'rubbing in' part, where the pieces of butter are combined with the flour, needs a delicate touch. Try to use just your (cool) fingertips so your (warm and sticky) palms stay clean.

 Lift your hands up to the rim of the bowl so that as the mixture falls back down into the bowl it gets aerated – this will make a lighter pastry.

 Don't use lots of flour for rolling out pastry as it will end up tough, dry and hard – if it feels soft and sticky put it back into the fridge for 15 minutes to firm up.

 Put a baking sheet into the oven to heat when baking a tart, flan or quiche with a wet filling. This will help the pastry base become crisp and dry and avoid the dreaded 'soggy bottom'.

SWEET SHORTCRUST PASTRY

Master home-made shortcrust pastry and then fill the light, crisp case with your favourite filling.

200g plain flour
2 tablespoons icing sugar
125g unsalted butter,
  cold from the fridge
about 3 tablespoons very cold
  water from the tap

YOU WILL ALSO NEED
✴ Large sieve ✴ large bowl for mixing
✴ table knife ✴ rolling pin ✴ 18cm
loose-based, deep flan tin ✴ fork
✴ baking paper ✴ baking beans
✴ baking sheet

Technique
Making pastry from scratch

1 Set the sieve over the mixing bowl and put the flour and icing sugar into it. Sift them into the bowl by gently tapping the sieve with your hand (sifting not only gets rid of any lumps but it adds a bit of air, which helps make the pastry light).

2 Cut the butter into tiny cubes. Add to the bowl and toss around with the table knife so they become coated with flour. Now cut the butter, in the bowl, into even tinier pieces by cutting through the mixture at random.

3 When the butter is about the size of small peas, put both your hands into the bowl and pick up a little of the butter/flour mix with your fingers only. Rub the mixture between your fingers and thumbs so the butter is squashed into the flour, then drops back down into the bowl (rubbing in)*. Keep doing this for a few minutes, then give the bowl a little shake – you should see any lumps you've missed. When all the lumps of butter have disappeared it's ready for the next stage.

4 Add the cold water and stir everything together with the table knife. When the mixture has started to come together in clumps of dough, use your hands to gather up the whole lot into a ball. If there are dry crumbs at the bottom of the bowl and the dough won't stick together, sprinkle over a teaspoon of cold water and gently mix it in; if the dough sticks to your hands or the bowl, sprinkle over a teaspoon of flour and mix it in. The dough should feel firm – not sticky or wet or dry and hard. Flatten the dough into a disc about 5cm thick, then wrap it in clingfilm. Chill in the fridge for 15 minutes.

Turn over the page

5 Sprinkle a little flour on the worktop, your hands and the rolling pin. Unwrap the pastry dough and set it in the middle of the worktop. Start rolling out the pastry in a forward and back motion, then side to side, sprinkling with a little more flour now and then to prevent it from sticking to the pin, until it is fairly round in shape and about 26cm in diameter.

6 Have your flan tin next to you. Sprinkle the rolling pin with a little more flour, then set the pin down on one edge of the pastry round and loosely roll up around the pin. Lift the pin up and over the flan tin, then slowly unroll the pastry so it drapes over the tin and hangs down over the sides.

7 Dip your fingers in a little flour so they don't stick to the pastry, then – really delicately – press the pastry onto the base of the tin (start in the centre and move out to the sides), pressing out air pockets and wrinkles.

8 Now for the sides. Flour your fingers again and gently press the pastry into the corners where the sides meet the base. Then gently press the pastry into each of the grooves in the tin – try not to stretch the pastry.

9 If there are tiny holes/tears/cracks, don't worry – just press the pastry back together again; any bigger holes can be patched with a scrap of the excess overhanging pastry and a dab of water.

10 When you think the pastry case looks good, roll the rolling pin over the top of the tin to chop off the overhanging pastry (save this for jam tarts, page 183). The edge will probably look thick and unattractive, so use your fingers to gently press the pastry back into the grooves and slightly higher than the rim of the tin (in case it shrinks during baking).

READY-ROLLED

You can use a ready-rolled shortcrust pastry sheet to make your tart. Take the pastry out of the fridge about 30 minutes before you want to use it. Gently unroll the pastry on the worktop and then follow this recipe from step 6.

Turn over the page

11 Prick the base of the pastry case in several places with the fork so it doesn't bubble up during baking, then chill it in the fridge for 20 minutes – this will help it to keep a good shape in the oven. Meanwhile, preheat the oven to 190°C/375°F/gas 5.

12 Cut a sheet of baking paper into a square with sides about 35cm. Crumple it up, then flatten it out again (this makes it more flexible and easier to use). Press it into the chilled pastry case so it completely lines the base and the sides and sticks up above the edge. Fill with ceramic baking beans (you can also use dried beans).

13 Carefully place the tin in the heated oven and bake the pastry case for 15 minutes – it will be set but only half-cooked (this is 'baking blind'*). Wearing oven gloves, take the tin out of the oven and set it on a heatproof surface. With great care lift out the paper with the beans (leave them to cool, then save for next time). The pastry will look soggy and damp.

14 Return the empty pastry case to the oven and bake for 10–12 minutes until the pastry has turned a very pale gold and looks dry. Remove and set on a heatproof surface. Turn down the oven to 180°C/350°F/gas 4. Put the baking sheet into the oven to heat up while you make the filling.

THINGS TO MAKE WITH YOUR PASTRY

Once you've made your sweet shortcrust pastry, there are loads of things you can turn it in to. The recipe on page 170 makes about 320g of pastry. Use this to create:

The rich and creamy Chocolate Tart on page 178

The colourful Raspberry Tart with a homemade custard filling on page 182

Jam Tarts to impress the Queen of Hearts (and Mary Berry) on page 183

The Summer Tart on page 188 – perfect for beginner bakers, no special tins required

Or turn to page 194 for homemade Mince Pies – Happy Christmas!

SAVOURY SHORTCRUST PASTRY

FOR A CHEESE AND HAM FILLING
125g thickly sliced lean ham
75g Cheddar cheese, grated
200ml single or whipping cream
2 eggs
small bunch of chives
freshly ground black pepper

YOU WILL ALSO NEED
✳ Baking sheet ✳ kitchen scissors
✳ grater ✳ measuring jug ✳ fork
or wire whisk

If you want to make a savoury tart, simply follow the recipe from page 177 but leave out the icing sugar. Then all you need is a basic egg filling, to which you can add your own flavour combos. To start you off, here is a recipe for a cheese and ham filling that turns your home-made savoury tart case into a classic quiche.

1 Snip the ham using kitchen scissors and scatter over the cooked pastry tart base. Sprinkle over the grated cheese.

2 Measure the cream into a measuring jug and crack the eggs into it. Mix everything together with a fork or wire whisk.

3 Put the cooked pastry case onto the hot baking sheet and pour in the egg mixture. Don't over fill or it will run over as it cooks and make a mess!

4 Bake the savoury tart for 30 minutes at 180°C/350°F/gas 4 until the filling is golden brown and puffed up. Using oven gloves, remove the tart from the oven and leave to cool for 15 minutes before removing from the tin (see page 181). Serve with a green salad and jacket potatoes.

Serves 8
CHOCOLATE TART

FOR THE PASTRY
1 x baked, sweet shortcrust
   pastry tart case (page 170)

FOR THE FILLING
100g bar dark chocolate
200ml double cream
   (not the extra-thick type)
2 eggs, at room temperature*
icing sugar, for dusting

YOU WILL ALSO NEED
✳ Baking sheet ✳ medium saucepan
✳ wooden spoon ✳ wide-necked
measuring jug ✳ small bowl
✳ plastic or rubber scraper

This is a proper treat to make for someone you love.

1 Follow the pastry recipe from page 170, then preheat the oven to 180°C/350°F/gas 4. Put the baking sheet in the oven while you make the filling.

2 Use the rolling pin to bash up the bar of chocolate, still in its wrapper. Pour the cream into the saucepan and warm over medium heat until it just starts to steam and small bubbles appear around the edge (this is simmering). Carefully take the pan off the heat.

3 Add the chocolate pieces to the warm cream. Give the pan a little shake so all the pieces of chocolate are covered with cream, then leave for a minute or so to soften. Gently stir with the wooden spoon until the chocolate has melted and the mixture is very smooth.

4 Break one egg into the measuring jug and separate* the second egg – you only need the yolk from the second egg. Add the yolk to the whole egg in the measuring jug. Wash your hands. Scrape the mixture into the jug and mix really well.

5 Wearing oven gloves, take the hot baking sheet out of the oven and set on a heatproof surface. Place the flan tin on the sheet, then pour in the chocolate filling.

6 Carefully return the flan tin (on the baking sheet) to the oven and bake for 20 minutes until the filling is slightly puffed and matt rather than shiny on top. Remove from the oven (with oven gloves on) and set on a heatproof surface. Leave until completely cold.

7 Lift up the flan tin and set it centrally on a tin of food – the side of the flan tin will drop down, leaving the tart on the metal base. If the pastry sticks a bit to the side of the tin, just gently loosen with a table knife.

8 Set the tart on a serving plate and sprinkle lightly with icing sugar. Eat at room temperature* the same day.

2

4

3

5

6

Serves 8
RASPBERRY TART

A pretty fruit tart, perfect for a special Sunday lunch in summer. Great with vanilla ice cream!

1 Follow the pastry recipe from page 170, then preheat the oven to 190°C/375°F/gas 5. Put the baking sheet in the oven while you make the filling.

2 Measure the cream in the measuring jug. Separate* the eggs and put the yolks into the measuring jug. (Keep the whites for another recipe.) Now wash your hands.

3 Add the sugar to the jug and whisk* everything together with the fork or whisk until the mixture looks creamy, with no streaks.

4 Wearing oven gloves, lift the hot baking sheet out of the oven and set it on a heatproof surface. Place the flan tin on the sheet. Slowly pour the egg mixture into the pastry case. Gently arrange the raspberries in a pretty pattern on top. Some may sink – it doesn't matter.

5 Carefully put the sheet back into the oven and bake for 20 minutes. To test if the tart is cooked, carefully give the baking sheet a little shake (with your oven gloves on of course). If the custard wobbles it needs a bit more time in the oven (test again in 3 minutes or so). Lift the cooked tart out of the oven and set it on a heatproof surface. Leave the tart to cool, then put it in the fridge to chill for 15 minutes.

6 Carefully remove the flan tin (page 181). Set the tart on a serving plate. Put a spoonful of icing sugar into the small sieve or tea strainer and shake it over the tart so it is lightly sprinkled. Serve immediately. Best the same or next day (store covered in the fridge).

FOR THE PASTRY
1 x baked sweet shortcrust
   pastry tart case (page 170)

FOR THE FILLING
125ml double cream
2 eggs
2 tablespoons caster sugar
150g fresh raspberries
icing sugar

YOU WILL ALSO NEED
✴ Baking sheet ✴ measuring jug
✴ small bowl ✴ fork or wire whisk
✴ small spoon ✴ small sieve or
tea strainer

Makes 12
JAM TARTS

1 batch sweet shortcrust pastry
(page 170) or a ready-made,
sweet shortcrust pastry sheet
(thawed, if frozen, and taken
out of the fridge about
30 minutes ahead)
plain flour, for dusting
6 tablespoons jam

YOU WILL ALSO NEED
✱ Round fluted or daisy cutter
about 7.5cm ✱ 12-hole bun or
mincepie tray ✱ small spoon
✱ small shaped cutters (optional)
✱ wire rack

A bun tray is really useful – you can make little jam
tarts, bakewells and mincepies as well as fairy cakes.
Jam tarts just need shortcrust pastry and your
favourite jam (firm-set jam works best). Finish them
with cut-out decorations from the pastry scraps.

1 Follow the pastry recipe from page 170 until step 5, then
preheat the oven to 180°C/350°F/gas 4.

2 Dip the round pastry cutter in flour, then carefully press
it (sharp edge down) onto the pastry, pushing down hard
enough to cut through it. Carefully cut 11 more circles in
the same way.

3 Lift out one circle and gently press it into one of the holes
in the bun tray with your fingers, smoothing out air bubbles
or wrinkles. Do the same with all the other circles. Leave the
scraps of pastry on the worktop.

4 Spoon a rounded teaspoon of jam into the middle of each
pastry case.

5 If you want to decorate the tarts, dip the small cutters
in flour, then press them into the pastry scraps and cut out
shapes. You can also cut short strips or stars with a small
knife. Gently set a small shape on top the jam in the centre
of each tart.

6 Place the tray in the heated oven and bake for about
15 minutes until the top edges of the tarts are golden
brown. Wearing oven gloves, remove the tray and set it
on a heatproof surface.

7 Leave to cool for 5 minutes, then carefully remove the tarts
from the tray (take care with this as the jam will be hot) and
set them on the wire rack. Leave until cold before eating.

Serves 5–6
CHICKEN AND SWEETCORN PIE

400g cooked chicken (or turkey)
  without skin or bones
3 spring onions
125g frozen sweetcorn
20g unsalted butter
2 tablespoons plain flour
350ml chicken stock
  (ready-made or using a cube)
4 tablespoons half-fat crème fraîche
freshly ground black pepper
320g ready-rolled puff pastry sheet,
  thawed if frozen (take it out of the
  fridge about 10 minutes ahead)
1 egg, lightly beaten*

YOU WILL ALSO NEED
* Large bowl for mixing * kitchen
scissors * medium saucepan
* wooden spoon * 1 litre pie dish
(about 21 x 15 x 5cm) * small bowl
* fork * pastry brush * rolling pin
* small sharp knife * baking sheet

A home-made pie is a real treat – a meal
everyone loves. For this chicken pie you need
some cold cooked chicken (or Christmas turkey),
vegetables from the freezer and a sauce you
make yourself. Your pie will look and smell
wonderful when you pull it out of the oven.

1 Use your hands to pull the cooked chicken meat into
shreds about the size of your little finger. Put into the
mixing bowl.

2 Trim the spring onions with kitchen scissors to get rid
of the hairy root ends and the tough dark green leaves at
the top. Give the spring onions a rinse under the cold tap
to wash off any grit, then snip them with the scissors into
thin rounds straight into the bowl with the chicken. Add
the frozen sweetcorn to the bowl.

3 Now make the sauce. Put the butter into the saucepan,
set over medium heat and leave it to melt for a few
seconds. Tip the flour into the pan and stir into the
butter with the wooden spoon to make a thick, smooth
mixture (this is called a 'roux'). Gradually pour in the
stock while stirring, and keep stirring until the mixture
thickens as it begins to boil (if there are lumps that you
can't get rid of, carefully move the pan off the heat and
whisk with a wire whisk for a minute).

Turn over the page

4 Turn down the heat and leave the sauce to boil for a minute, stirring once or twice to stop it sticking to the bottom of the pan. Carefully remove from the heat and stir in the crème fraîche. When the sauce is smooth, add the chicken mixture and 3 or 4 grinds of black pepper. Mix everything together. Spoon the mixture into the pie dish.

5 Unroll the pastry on the worktop, keeping it on its plastic sheet, and flatten it out with your hands. With the scissors cut a strip 1cm wide from each long side.

6 Dip the pastry brush into the beaten* egg, then brush onto the rim of the pie dish, to make it damp. Set the strips of pastry on the rim and press them on with your fingers so they stick. Brush the pastry strips with egg.

7 Peel the rest of the pastry sheet from the plastic, then loosely roll around the rolling pin and lift it over the top of the pie dish. Unroll the pastry so it completely covers the top of the dish. Very gently press the pastry onto the damp pastry rim – don't stretch the pastry, just ease it in place. When it is all firmly stuck down, trim off the pastry that's hanging over the edge of the dish using kitchen scissors.

8 Chill the pie in the fridge for 15 minutes so the pastry can firm up and relax a bit (this will help prevent it from shrinking in the oven). Meanwhile, preheat the oven to 190°C/375°F/gas 5.

9 Cut a small slit about 2cm long in the centre of the pastry lid so steam can escape during baking. Brush the lid with beaten* egg to give it a shiny glaze. You can cut shapes or letters out of the pastry scraps to decorate the pie. Press them onto the damp surface, then paint them with a little egg too.

10 Set the pie dish on the baking sheet and bake in the heated oven for 35–40 minutes until the pastry is golden brown. Wearing oven gloves, remove the baking sheet with the pie on it and set on a heatproof surface. Eat the pie while it's hot, with green vegetables.

FISH PIE

Replace the chicken with flaked cooked fish (salmon works well) and use fish or veg stock instead of chicken stock. You could also add 1–2 chopped, hard-boiled eggs and a few sprigs fresh parsley, snipped up.

SUMMER TART

1 batch sweet shortcrust pastry (page 170) or a ready-made, sweet shortcrust pastry sheet (thawed, if frozen, and taken out of the fridge about 30 minutes ahead)
3 medium-sized sweet eating apples
100g blueberries
2 tablespoons caster sugar, plus extra for sprinkling
½ teaspoon ground cinnamon

YOU WILL ALSO NEED

✶ Small sharp knife ✶ kitchen scissors (optional) ✶ rolling pin ✶ baking sheet, lined with baking paper ✶ vegetable peeler ✶ chopping board ✶ large bowl for mixing ✶ colander ✶ large spoon ✶ pastry brush ✶ small spoon

PEAR TART

Replace the apples with 3 firm pears. Sprinkle 2 tablespoons toasted flaked almonds, or pine nuts, onto the centre of the pastry circle before you heap the fruit on top.

A really easy apple and blueberry tart. Serve with warm custard or vanilla icecream.

1 Follow the pastry recipe from page 170 until step 5, then preheat the oven to 200°C/400°F/gas 6. Arrange the pastry sheet on the baking sheet, pressing it lightly with your hands to flatten out any kinks.

2 If using a ready-made pastry sheet, find a round plate or a pan lid that's 25cm in diameter and set it on top of the pastry, in the centre of the baking sheet. Cut around it with the knife. Remove the trimmings and then chill the pastry disc while you prepare the filling.

3 Peel the apples and put them on the chopping board and cut them into quarters. Cut out the cores. Cut each quarter into 6 slices and put into the mixing bowl.

4 Tip the blueberries into the colander and rinse under cold running water. Then shake the colander well so the blueberries are as dry as possible. Tip them into the mixing bowl. Add the sugar and cinnamon and mix everything together very well with the large spoon.

5 Take the baking sheet out of the fridge. Spoon the fruit into the centre of the pastry circle to make a neat mound. Leave 5cm of the pastry uncovered all around it. Fold the uncovered pastry up around the fruit in gathers.

6 Wet the pastry brush under the cold tap, then brush water over the pastry border. Sprinkle the border with a little caster sugar.

7 Carefully place the baking sheet in the heated oven and bake for 35 minutes until the pastry is golden brown. Wearing oven gloves, remove the sheet from the oven and set on a heatproof surface. Leave to cool for 10 minutes, then slide the tart onto a serving platter. Eat warm as soon as possible.

Makes 20
SAUSAGE ROLLS

320g ready-rolled puff pastry
   sheet, thawed if frozen
   (take it out of the fridge
   about 10 minutes ahead)
450g favourite sausages
1 egg
pinch of salt

YOU WILL ALSO NEED
✸ Kitchen scissors ✸ 2 small
bowls ✸ fork ✸ pastry brush
✸ small sharp knife ✸ baking
sheet, lined with baking paper
✸ fish slice ✸ wire rack.

Perfect for a picnic, this popular pastry snack
is really easy to make yourself.

1 Preheat the oven to 220°C/425°F/gas 7. Unroll the pastry on
the worktop, keeping it on its plastic sheet, and gently flatten
it out with your hand. Using scissors, cut the pastry sheet in
half down its length to make 2 strips each about 12 x 36cm.

2 Squeeze the sausages out of their skins into a bowl (throw
away the empty skins). Divide the sausagemeat in half. Pick
up one portion and shape it into one long sausage the same
length as your strips of pastry.

3 With the handle of the fork, draw a line down the centre of
one strip of pastry (don't cut through it). Now draw another
line halfway between this and the pastry edge. Set the giant
sausage on this second line. Do the same with the other
portion of sausagemeat and the other pastry strip. Wash
your hands after touching the sausages.

4 Break the egg into the other small bowl (wash your hands
again). Add the salt and lightly beat* with the fork. Brush all
the long pastry edges with beaten egg. Fold the pastry over
the sausagemeat to cover it completely – make sure the long
edges meet neatly. Press the edges together very firmly with
your fingers to seal. Press down on the seam (all along the
length) with the back of the fork to give a stripey pattern.

5 Cut each of the long rolls across into 10 equal pieces and
transfer them to the lined baking sheet. Brush the top and
sides of each roll with beaten egg. Place in the oven and
bake for 15–20 minutes until golden brown.

6 Wearing oven gloves, remove the sheet from the oven
and set on a heatproof surface. With the fish slice, carefully
transfer the hot rolls to the wire rack and leave to cool for
at least 10 minutes before eating. Best the same day.

BAKED VEGGIE SAMOSAS

3 spring onions
2 x 2cm chunks fresh root ginger
1 medium potato (about 200g)
½ teaspoon mild curry paste,
    or to taste
200ml vegetable stock
    (made from a cube) or water
200g frozen mixed vegetables
    (from a pack of peas, sweetcorn,
    diced carrots and green beans)
8 sheets filo pastry, each about
    25.5 x 48cm (250g box), thawed
    if frozen (take out of the fridge
    but keep in its wrapping so it
    doesn't dry out)
3–4 tablespoons rapeseed or
    vegetable oil, for brushing

YOU WILL ALSO NEED
✴ Chopping board ✴ small sharp
knife ✴ small spoon ✴ grater
✴ vegetable peeler ✴ medium non-
stick frying pan ✴ wooden spoon
✴ pastry brush ✴ kitchen scissors
✴ non-stick baking sheet, lightly
brushed with oil or lined
with baking paper

These spicy veg-filled samosas are made with filo pastry sheets and baked, not deep-fried in the traditional way. They're great party snacks.

1 Put the spring onions on the chopping board and carefully trim off the hairy root ends and the dark green coarse tops. Rinse the onions under the tap to get rid of any grit and dirt. Give them a good shake in the sink so they are not too wet, then slice them into rounds about 3mm thick. Push them to one side of the board.

2 Use the small spoon to scrape the beige peel off the root ginger so you can see the yellow inside. Carefully grate the ginger onto the board using the fine-hole side of the grater. Push to the side with the onions. Peel the potato, then cut it on the board into 1cm chunks.

3 Put the spring onions, ginger and potato into the frying pan. Add the curry paste and stock or water, then set the pan over medium heat and stir gently with the wooden spoon until the mixture starts to boil. Turn down the heat so the liquid is just boiling gently with tiny bubbles (this is simmering) and cook for 15 minutes, stirring every few minutes.

4 Carefully lift the pan off the heat and set it on a heatproof surface. Wait for the bubbling to stop, then gently add the frozen vegetables and stir them in to mix. Return the pan to the heat and bring back to the boil.

5 Cook for about 5 minutes until the vegetables feel soft when you prod them with the wooden spoon and all the liquid has evaporated. If the vegetables still feel hard or you can see liquid in the pan, cook for 2–3 more minutes. Once the vegetables are soft and look fairly dry, remove from the heat and leave to cool.

6 Preheat the oven to 200°C/400°F/gas 6. When the vegetable mix is cold, taste a small amount on a teaspoon. If you think it needs more spice, stir in ¼ teaspoon more curry paste (or you could add a few grinds of black pepper).

7 Carefully unwrap the filo on a clean worktop. Have the vegetable filling close by. Peel off the top sheet of filo and lay it in front of you (cover the rest of the filo with a clean and slightly damp tea towel or a large sheet of clingfilm so it doesn't dry out). Brush the filo sheet very lightly with oil, then cut it lengthways into 3 long strips using kitchen scissors (take care as filo tears easily).

8 Spoon 2 tablespoons of the veg mixture in a heap near the top of one strip, leaving about 2cm of pastry uncovered at the top and on either side. Now start folding the pastry strip into a triangle: take the top right hand corner and fold it down diagonally to the left so it covers the filling. Push in any escaped vegetables, then take the point at the top left and fold it down diagonally to the right. Keep folding the pastry over like this until you get to the bottom of the strip of filo.

9 Set the triangle on the prepared baking sheet and lightly brush with oil. Fill and fold the other 2 strips in the same way, and keep making the samosas until you have used up all the filo and vegetables.

10 Place in the heated oven and bake for about 20 minutes until golden brown. Wearing oven gloves, remove the sheet from the oven and set on a heatproof surface. Leave to cool for 5 minutes. Eat warm as soon as possible.

Makes 12
MINCE PIES

2 batches shortcrust pastry
(page 170) or 2 ready-made,
sweet shortcrust pastry sheets
(thawed, if frozen and taken
out of the fridge about
30 minutes ahead)
Plain flour for dusting
About ½ x 410g jar mincemeat
Caster sugar or icing sugar
for dusting

YOU WILL ALSO NEED
✶ Round fluted or plain cutters
about 6.5cm and 7.5cm ✶ 12-hole
bun or mincepie tray ✶ small
spoon ✶ small shaped cutters
(optional) ✶ pastry brush ✶ small
bowl ✶ wire rack ✶ small sieve
or tea strainer

It's easy to bake a batch of these traditional sweet
little pies – plus they make the house smell just
like Christmas!

1 Follow the pastry recipe from page 170 until step 5, making
double the quantity. Preheat the oven to 180°C/350°F/gas 4.
If using 2 ready-made pastry sheets, gently unroll one of the
sheets onto the worktop, leaving it on the plastic sheet. Dip
the larger, 7.5cm, cutter in flour then carefully press it (sharp
edge down) onto the pastry, pushing down hard enough to
cut through it to stamp out a circle. Carefully cut out 11 more
circles in the same way.

2 Lift out one circle and gently press it into one of the holes
in the bun tray with your fingers, pressing out and smoothing
out any wrinkles or air bubbles. Do the same with all the
other circles.

3 Give the jar of mincemeat a stir to soften the mixture, then
spoon about 1 ½ teaspoons mincemeat into the centre of each
pastry base.

4 Unroll the second sheet of pastry as you did before and this
time cut out 12 circles using the smaller, 6.5cm, cutter. Add
the pastry trimmings to the first batch and wrap tightly and
chill. Dip the pastry brush in a small bowl of cold water, shake
off the excess water so the brush is just damp, then brush the
edges of each pastry lid with water.

5 Turn the circles upside down and gently set one (damp side
down) on top of each base. Press the edges together very
firmly so they seal (you don't want the filling to bubble out).
Make a small hole in the centre of each lid with a cocktail
stick so the steam can escape.

6 Bake in the heated oven for 20 to 25 minutes until the
pastry is golden. Leave to cool for 5 minutes in the tray then
carefully lift out onto a wire rack and sprinkle with sugar.

7 Eat warm or at room temperature. When cold, pack into
an airtight container and eat within 3 days.

Learn to Bake

PUDDINGS

Egg whites for meringues will whisk up better if they are at room temperature rather than cold from the fridge.

 Double check your bowl before you start. You'll get a better meringue – more volume – if the bowl is spotlessly clean. A speck of fat or grease will mean less froth, so double check before you begin.

 Add a pinch of (acidic) cream of tartar, a drop of lemon juice or a pinch of salt to egg whites as you start to whisk. This will help the structure of the foam and make a more stable meringue.

 Stand the mixing bowl on a damp cloth (or use a bowl with a non-slip rubber base) so it doesn't wobble or tip over as you mix and beat.

 The 'stiff' peak test. You'll know when the whites are ready when you can hold the bowl upside down over someone's head without it dripping . . .

 Don't throw away spare egg whites. Freeze them in small containers (mark the quantity). Defrost thoroughly and use at room temperature for soufflés and meringues.

STRAWBERRY PAVLOVA

3 eggs, at room temperature, whites and yolks separated* into 2 bowls
pinch of salt
175g caster sugar
2 teaspoons cornflour
½ teaspoon vanilla extract
1 teaspoon white wine vinegar

FOR THE TOPPING

250ml whipping cream, cold from the fridge
350g fresh strawberries

YOU WILL ALSO NEED

✳ Baking sheet ✳ baking paper ✳ large bowl for mixing ✳ hand-held electric mixer ✳ large sieve ✳ medium bowl ✳ medium spoon ✳ plastic or rubber scraper ✳ large metal spoon ✳ chopping board ✳ small sharp knife

Pavlova was named after a famous Russian ballerina – Anna Pavlova – because the base is supposed to look like a crisp, white ballet tutu.

1 Preheat the oven to 140°C/275°F/gas 1. Set the baking sheet on a piece of baking paper and cut around it so you have a rectangle of paper that fits exactly. Put a small dot of butter into each corner of the baking sheet, then press the paper onto the sheet – the butter will hold it in place.

2 You only need the egg whites for this recipe, so save the yolks for another recipe. Whisk* the whites in the mixing bowl with the electric mixer on medium speed for about 20 seconds until they look frothy. Add the salt and whisk on full speed until the whites form soft peaks*.

3 Sift* the sugar and cornflour into the medium bowl. Sprinkle a spoonful of the sugar mixture over the egg whites and whisk in until it disappears (about 5 seconds). Keep adding the sugar mixture in this way until you have used half the sugar.

4 Sprinkle the vanilla and vinegar over the meringue mixture, then whisk for 5 seconds. Scrape down the sides of the bowl. Sift the rest of the sugar/cornflour mixture over the bowl of meringue (so it gets a second sifting).

5 With the edge of the large metal spoon, fold* in the sugar mixture, gently cutting down through the meringue. Keep folding until the sugar and whites are thoroughly combined and you can't see any streaks.

Turn over the page

6 Spoon the meringue mixture into a pile on the lined baking sheet. Gently spread it out with the scraper to a circle about 23cm across. Carefully make a shallow hollow in the centre, pushing the meringue out to make a surrounding edge about 6cm high and wide.

7 Carefully place in the heated oven and bake for about 1 ¼ hours until the meringue feels very crisp to a light touch. Carefully open the oven door after 1 hour of baking and check the colour – if the meringue is starting to turn golden, turn down the oven to 120°C/250°F/gas ½ for the rest of the cooking time. Turn off the oven and leave the pavlova to cool inside with the door closed. When the oven is cold, remove the pavlova.

8 To make the topping, put the cream into the washed mixing bowl and whip* with the electric mixer until thick enough to form a soft peak when the whisk is lifted out of the bowl.

9 Wipe the strawberries with kitchen paper to make sure they are clean (or rinse and dry them if necessary). Pull out or cut away the green stalk ends (this is hulling the strawberries). Put them on the chopping board and carefully cut large strawberries into quarters and small strawberries in half. Stir about 100g of the chopped strawberries into the cream with the large metal spoon.

10 Peel off the lining from the pavlova and put it on a serving plate. Spoon the cream into the centre hollow of the pavlova. Scatter the remaining 250g chopped strawberries over the cream and finish with a dusting of icing sugar, just before serving.

CHOCOLATE PAVLOVA

Melt 75g dark chocolate, then leave to cool while you make the meringue mixture as in the main recipe. After folding in all the sugar mixture, slowly pour the melted chocolate over the meringue mixture and gently stir it through as though you were drawing the number 8 – you want to see large chocolate streaks against the white meringue. Then continue with the rest of the recipe.

Serves 6–8
LEMON MERINGUE PIE

FOR THE PASTRY CASE
1 x baked, sweet shortcrust
  pastry tart case (page 170)

FOR THE LEMON FILLING
2 unwaxed lemons
3 tablespoons cornflour
3 eggs, at room temperature*
60g caster sugar
30g unsalted butter, cut into 1cm pieces

FOR THE TOPPING
150g caster sugar

YOU WILL ALSO NEED
✳ Rolling pin ✳ 18cm loose-based,
deep flan tin ✳ fork ✳ baking paper
✳ baking beans ✳ baking sheet
✳ lemon zester or grater ✳ medium
heatproof bowl ✳ chopping board
✳ small sharp knife ✳ lemon squeezer
✳ wooden spoon ✳ medium saucepan
✳ large bowl for mixing ✳ plastic or
rubber scraper ✳ hand-held electric
mixer ✳ 2 medium spoons

Technique
Making meringue

This has to be everyone's favourite pie, and it's
good to know how it's put together – pastry case,
lemon filling (made in a pan) and whisked egg
white meringue topping. A great combination!

1 Follow the pastry recipe from page 170, then preheat
the oven to 190°C/375°F/gas 5. Put the baking sheet in
the oven while you make the filling and topping.

2 Grate the zest from the lemons into the heatproof bowl*
(page 22). Put the lemons on the chopping board and cut
them in half. Squeeze out the juice and add to the bowl.
Spoon the cornflour into the bowl. Stir everything
together with the wooden spoon until smooth.

3 Pour 175ml water into the saucepan. Set it over medium
heat and bring to the boil, then turn off the heat. Wearing
an oven glove, lift the pan off the heat and pour the water
into the bowl, stirring the mixture with your other hand
(this may be a two-person job).

4 When everything is combined, pour it back into the
pan. Set over medium heat and stir with the wooden
spoon until the mixture thickens, changes colour (from
milky white to translucent) and comes to the boil. As
soon as it starts to bubble, turn off the heat. Keep stirring
for a minute, then – oven gloves on – set the pan on a
heatproof surface.

5 Separate the eggs*; put the yolks into the saucepan
(wash your hands). Add the sugar to the pan and stir
until combined. Add the butter and stir until it has melted
and disappeared. Scrape the mixture into the pastry
case (still in the tin) and spread evenly.

Turn over the page

6 Now make the topping. Set the bowl of egg whites on a damp cloth and whisk them with the electric mixer until thick and snowy-looking and they will form soft peaks*.Sprinkle a heaped tablespoon of the sugar over the egg whites and whisk in for 5 seconds. Slowly add the rest of the sugar in the same way, whisking, to make stiff peaks*.

7 Spoon the meringue mixture on top of the lemon filling in the pastry case – spread it evenly to cover the filling. Use the spoon to make swirls in the meringue.

8 Carefully set the flan tin on the hot baking sheet in the oven and bake for 15 minutes until the meringue is lightly browned. Wearing oven gloves, remove the baking sheet and set on a heatproof surface. Leave to cool completely.

9 Lift up the flan tin and set it centrally on a tin of food – the side of the flan tin will drop down, leaving the pie on the metal base (page 179). Store in a covered container in the fridge – take out an hour before serving. Best eaten within 2 days.

Makes 4
LEMONY SOUFFLÉS

FOR THE DISHES
20g unsalted butter, at room
    temperature
4 teaspoons caster sugar

FOR THE SOUFFLÉS
4 eggs, at room temperature*
225ml ready-made creamy
    vanilla custard
2 unwaxed lemons
4 tablespoons caster sugar

TO FINISH
1–2 tablespoons icing sugar

YOU WILL ALSO NEED
✲ 4 ramekin dishes (about 9cm/175ml
capacity) ✲ baking sheet ✲ large bowl
✲ medium bowl ✲ lemon zester or
grater ✲ chopping board ✲ small sharp
knife ✲ lemon squeezer ✲ plastic or
rubber scraper ✲ hand-held electric
mixer ✲ large metal spoon ✲ small
sieve or tea strainer

Here's a very quick and easy way to make
ultra-light baked lemon soufflés – all you need
is a tub of ready-made rich and creamy vanilla
custard plus eggs, sugar and lemons. If you've
tried making meringues then you'll have fun
creating these 'breaths of air'.

1 Preheat the oven to 220°C/425°F/gas 7. Grease the
inside of the ramekins with the soft butter on a scrap of
kitchen paper. Put a teaspoon of sugar in each ramekin,
then tip and rotate so the sugar coats the side as well as
the base. This coating helps the soufflé mixture to rise
up in the dish during baking (instead of sliding down).
Set the ramekins on the baking sheet.

2 Separate 2 of the eggs*; put the yolks into the medium
bowl. Separate the remaining 2 eggs, putting the whites
into the large bowl. (Save the 2 yolks in a container in the
fridge for another recipe). Now wash your hands.

3 Spoon the custard into the bowl with the 2 egg yolks.
Grate the zest from the lemons* into the bowl.

4 Put the lemons on the chopping board and cut them
in half. Squeeze out the juice, then pour the juice into the
custard bowl. Stir the yolks, custard and lemon zest and
juice together with the scraper until smooth and
thoroughly combined.

Turn over the page

Preparing the ramekins

Folding in the meringue

5 Whisk the 4 egg whites with the electric mixer on high speed until thick – if the whisk is lifted out of the bowl, the mixture should form a soft peak*. Sprinkle the caster sugar over the egg whites. Whisk for about a minute until the meringue mixture is thicker and glossier and stands in stiff peaks* when the whisk is lifted.

6 Using the large metal spoon, take a scoop of the meringue and stir it into the custard mixture – this will lighten the custard enough to make it easy to fold in* the rest of the meringue (it's harder to combine a thin mixture with a thick mixture)*.

7 Now add the rest of the meringue to the custard. With the edge of the large metal spoon, fold* the meringue into the custard. Keep folding very gently until just combined and you can't see any large clumps of meringue – but don't over-do it and knock out all the air you've beaten in.

8 Gently spoon the soufflé mixture into the prepared ramekins on the baking sheet. Run the tip of the knife around the top inside edge of each ramekin, just to loosen the mixture from the sides – this will help it to rise better.

9 Place in the heated oven and bake for 10–12 minutes until puffed up and the tops are turning golden – the soufflés will just wobble slightly in the middle when you gently shake the baking sheet.

10 Wearing oven gloves, remove the baking sheet from the oven and set on a heatproof surface. Quickly sift* a little icing sugar over the soufflés and serve instantly!

Makes about 18
DROP SCONES

100g self-raising flour
1 egg, at room temperature*
150ml milk, at room temperature*
1 teaspoon golden syrup
1 teaspoon caster sugar
25g unsalted butter, plus about
   15g for cooking
175g small blueberries

TO SERVE
blueberries
golden syrup or maple syrup

YOU WILL ALSO NEED
✳ Large sieve ✳ large bowl for mixing
✳ small saucepan or microwave-safe
bowl/cup ✳ wire whisk ✳ medium
non-stick frying pan ✳ tablespoon
✳ fish slice

A wonderful, almost instant hot snack for teatime or breakfast. If made without blueberries, serve with butter and jam, or honey, or peanut butter.

1 Sift* the flour into the mixing bowl. Add the egg, milk, golden syrup and sugar.

2 Put the 25g butter in the saucepan and melt over very low heat (or melt in the microwave in 10-second bursts). Pour the melted butter into the mixing bowl. Stir with the whisk to combine, then whisk* briskly to make a thick, smooth batter. Gently stir in the blueberries.

3 Holding the 15g butter in a small piece of kitchen paper, rub it over the base of the frying pan to lightly grease it. Set the pan over medium heat and warm for 2 minutes. Move the bowl of batter next to the stove, and have a plate ready for the cooked scones.

4 Now you need to test if the pan is hot enough. Drop a small spoonful of the batter into the hot pan – it should sizzle nicely and start to set. If it doesn't, leave the pan to heat up for a minute or so more and test again.

5 When your pan's ready, you can start cooking the pancakes. Use a rounded tablespoon measure of batter for each one, dropping it into the pan. You should be able to fit 3 pancakes in the pan, spaced well apart.

Turn over the page

6 Leave to cook for 2 minutes until the top surface looks set, rather than shiny and wet, and bubbles that appeared have burst.

7 Use the fish slice to carefully lift the edge of one pancake to check the colour of the underside. When it is golden brown, slide the fish slice under the scone and flip it over. Cook the other side for 2 minutes, then lift the scone out of the pan onto the plate and wrap in a clean tea towel.

8 Continue making scones until all the batter is used up. If the scones start to stick, put on your oven gloves, then take the pan off the heat and set it on a heatproof surface. Leave to cool for a couple of minutes. Take a large pad of folded kitchen paper with a little extra butter on it and wipe over the base of the pan to clean off any stuck-on bits and add a new layer of grease (take care as the pan will be hot). Then reheat the pan and continue cooking the scones. Serve the scones with extra blueberries, if you like, and the syrup.

PEANUT BUTTER SCONES

To make plain scones, leave out the caster sugar and blueberries. If you want to eat these cold later, or toasted the next day, cover them lightly with a clean tea towel so they don't dry out as they cool. Spread warm plain drop scones with your favourite peanut butter, then layer up in stacks of 3. Pour maple syrup over and eat with a knife and fork.

Serves 6
APRICOT CRUMBLE

FOR THE CRUMBLE TOPPING
100g plain flour
75g porridge oats
100g demerara sugar
100g unsalted butter,
   cold from the fridge

FOR THE FRUIT MIXTURE
8 large fresh apricots
200g fresh raspberries

YOU WILL ALSO NEED
✷ Large bowl for mixing ✷ table knife
✷ colander ✷ chopping board ✷ small
sharp knife ✷ large shallow baking
dish (about 1.5 litre capacity)

APPLE CRUMBLE

When apricots are out of season
use cooking apples instead – you
will need 2 large or 3 medium
Bramley apples; peel them, then
cut into quarters. Cut out the
cores. Cut each quarter into slices
about 1cm thick. Put into a large
mixing bowl and sprinkle over 3
tablespoons demerara sugar. Add
150g blackberries, raspberries or
loganberries and 1 tablespoon
water, then gently stir together.
Spoon into the baking dish, then
continue as in the main recipe.

A crunchy topping works well with a juicy fruit
filling. This pudding is easy to put together and
is great served with custard or vanilla ice cream.

1 Preheat the oven to 180°C/350°F/gas 4. To make the
crumble topping, put the flour, oats and sugar into the
mixing bowl. Mix with your hands until combined.

2 Cut the butter into fingernail-size pieces and add to
the bowl. Using the table knife, toss the bits of butter in
the flour mixture to coat them. Rub in* the flour mixture
and butter together until the mixture looks like lumpy
porridge with a few pea-sized lumps (page 171).

3 Put the apricots on the chopping board and cut them
in half along what looks like a seam running around the
fruit. Twist the fruit to separate it into halves and lift out
the stone. Cut each apricot half in half.

4 Spread the quartered apricots in the baking dish.
Scatter the raspberries evenly over the top. Sprinkle with
1 tablespoon of water. Scatter the crumble topping over
the fruit – don't press it down – to make an even layer.

5 Carefully place in the heated oven and bake for about
35 minutes until the top is golden brown and the fruit
juices are bubbling up around the edges of the dish.
Wearing oven gloves, remove the dish from the oven
and set on a heatproof surface. Leave to cool for about
15 minutes before eating.

6 Any leftover crumble can be covered and kept in
a cool spot overnight. Eat next day at room temperature
or gently warm through in the oven (preheat it to
160°C/325°F/gas 3) for about 10 minutes.

THE BEST BAKED CHEESECAKE

FOR THE BISCUIT CRUST
150g digestive biscuits (10 or 11)
50g unsalted butter

FOR THE FILLING
600g full-fat cream cheese
150ml soured cream
3 eggs
150g caster sugar
½ teaspoon vanilla extract
1 unwaxed lemon

FOR THE TOPPING
150ml soured cream
1 tablespoon caster sugar
½ teaspoon vanilla extract

YOU WILL ALSO NEED
✳ Plastic bag ✳ rolling pin ✳ large bowl for mixing ✳ small saucepan or microwave-safe cup ✳ wooden spoon ✳ 20.5cm springclip tin, greased with butter ✳ baking sheet ✳ medium spoon ✳ lemon zester or grater ✳ hand-held electric mixer ✳ plastic or rubber scraper ✳ small bowl

Crisp and crunchy biscuit bases are quicker and easier to make than pastry, and work best with silky-smooth, rich and creamy fillings. This one has a touch of lemon and of vanilla. You can add some fruit on top if you like.

1 Preheat the oven to 180°C/350°F/gas 4. Put the biscuits into the plastic bag and screw up the end so nothing can escape, then bash the bag with the rolling pin until you have a bag full of crumbs. Tip into the mixing bowl.

2 Melt the butter in the saucepan over low heat (or melt in the microwave in 10-second bursts). Pour the butter into the mixing bowl and stir into the crumbs. When all the crumbs seem to be coated in butter (they will look darker than they did), tip them into the greased tin set on the baking sheet.

3 The crumbs need to be compressed into a firm case for the filling – you will need about a third of them for the side and the rest for the base. Push the crumbs for the side towards the edge of the tin. Spread out the crumbs remaining on the base so they are fairly evenly distributed, then press them down firmly with the back of the medium spoon to make a firm, even layer.

4 With the back of the spoon, gently press the crumbs at the edge against the side of the tin, easing them about halfway up. Once the crumb side looks fairly even in height and thickness, press firmly all around again with the back of the spoon – make sure the angle where the base meets the sides is 90 degrees.

Turn over the page

SUMMER FRUITS

Pile 400g mixed berries –
strawberries, raspberries, dessert
blackberries, loganberries – in the
middle just before serving. Then
sift icing sugar on top.

BLUEBERRY CHEESECAKE

Add some blueberries. Make up
the topping mixture, grating in
the zest of 1 unwaxed lemon. Stir
well, then spread over the baked
cheesecake. Arrange 200g
blueberries over the topping,
then bake and finish.

FLAVOURED CRUST

Use 150g gingersnaps or
chocolate sandwich biscuits
instead of plain digestives.

5 Place in the heated oven and bake for 5 minutes.
Wearing oven gloves, remove the sheet from the oven
and set on a heatproof surface. Don't turn off the oven.

6 Now, make the filling. Put the cream cheese, soured
cream, eggs, sugar and vanilla into the mixing bowl.
Grate the zest from the lemon* into the bowl.

7 Mix everything together with the electric mixer.
Use low speed at first to soften the cream cheese and
break up the eggs. Scrape down the bowl, then beat on
medium speed until the mixture is smooth and creamy.

8 Pour and scrape the mixture into the tin and spread it
evenly – it will come slightly above the biscuit crust rim.
Carefully set the tin, still on the baking sheet, in the oven
and bake for 40 minutes.

9 Wearing oven gloves, carefully remove the baking
sheet and set it on a heatproof surface. The cheesecake
will have a slight wobble when you gently shake the
sheet, but the surface should be set and not damp-
looking. Leave to cool for 5 minutes.

10 Meanwhile, make the topping. Put the soured
cream, sugar and vanilla into the small bowl and stir
with the scraper for a minute until smooth. Tip onto
the cheesecake and gently spread over the surface.

11 With oven gloves back on, place the cheesecake in
the oven to bake for a further 15 minutes. Remove it from
the oven and set on a heatproof surface. There should
now be only a slight wobble (the cheesecake will keep
on cooking for a while after it comes out of the oven).

12 Loosen the cheesecake in the tin* (this helps to stop
to cracking as it cools and contracts). Leave until cold.
Cover the tin with clingfilm and chill for 6 hours
(overnight if possible) before you unclip the side of the
tin and remove it. Store in a covered container in the
fridge for up to 5 days.

Makes 4
CHOC HOT POTS

100g bar dark chocolate, broken up
100g bar milk chocolate, broken up
50g unsalted butter,
   at room temperature*
80g caster sugar
1 teaspoon vanilla extract
3 eggs, at room temperature*
35g plain flour
1 tablespoon icing sugar,
   for sprinkling

YOU WILL ALSO NEED
✱ Baking sheet ✱ baking paper
✱ 4 ramekins or individual baking
dishes (about 9cm /175ml capacity),
greased with butter ✱ kitchen
scissors ✱ rolling pin ✱ medium
heatproof bowl ✱ small saucepan
✱ plastic or rubber scraper ✱ large
bowl for mixing ✱ large sieve ✱ hand-
held electric mixer ✱ medium spoon
✱ small sieve or tea strainer

Individual hot chocolate puddings with a molten choc middle – wonderful with cold vanilla ice cream! They're made with an all-in-one cake mixture plus a lot of melted chocolate.

1 Preheat the oven to 200°C/400°F/gas 6. Put the baking sheet into the oven to heat. Fold a sheet of baking paper into 4. Set a ramekin on top and draw around it. Cut out the 4 circles and press one into the base of each dish.

2 Put the dark and milk chocolate into the heatproof bowl. Melt gently* until smooth. Leave to cool.

3 Put the soft butter, sugar, vanilla and eggs into the mixing bowl. Sift* the flour into the bowl. Whisk* with the electric mixer on low to medium speed for a couple of minutes to make a very smooth, thick mixture. Scrape the melted chocolate into the bowl and whisk on low speed for a minute until you can't see any streaks.

4 Spoon the mixture into the prepared ramekins so they are evenly filled (they will be about half full). Wearing oven gloves, set the ramekins on the hot baking sheet in the oven and bake for 12 minutes.

5 To test if they are cooked, put on oven gloves again, then carefully take the sheet out of the oven and set it on a heatproof surface. Gently press the middle of one of the little puds (take care as it will be hot!). If it feels just firm, the centre will be gooey. If you want a more spongey pud without a gooey centre, bake for 3 more minutes or until the pudding feels firm when pressed.

6 With oven gloves on, carefully upturn a ramekin on each serving plate. Lift off the ramekin and peel off the paper discs. Sprinkle with icing sugar, then serve.

INDEX

ALSO AVAILABLE FROM
The Great British Bake Off

How to achieve baking perfection at home, with foolproof recipes and simple step-by-step masterclasses based on Mary and Paul's Technical Challenges.

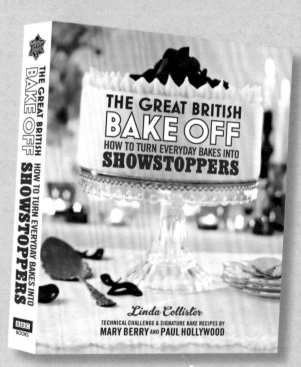

Baking doesn't have to be complicated to be 'showstopping'. Inspired by the Showstopper Challenge, here are bakes that will both turn heads and make mouths water.

Recipes from your favourite show, now in your pocket! Download The Great British Bake Off app and get 50 amazing recipes.